Basic Projects
in
Wildlife Watching

Basic Projects
in
Wildlife Watching

*Learn more about wild birds and
animals through your own
first-hand experience*

Sam Fadala

Wildlife photography by John Fadala

Stackpole Books

Published by
STACKPOLE BOOKS
Cameron and Kelker Streets
P.O. Box 1831
Harrisburg, PA 17105

Printed in the United States of America

10 9 8 7 6 5 4 3 2 1

Cover design by Tracy Patterson

Library of Congress Cataloging-in-Publication Data

Fadala, Sam, 1939–
    Basic projects in wildlife watching : learn more about wild birds and animals through your own first-hand experience / Sam Fadala : wildlife photography by John Fadala.
        p.   cm.
    Includes index.
    ISBN 0-8117-2248-1
    1. Wildlife watching.   I. Title.
    QL60.F36   1989
    599′.007′8 — dc19

88-31241
CIP

For Nicole, who watches wildlife with wide-eyed wonder, and who, with childlike wisdom, has taught me to see the same way

Contents

The Why of Wildlife Watching

Fascination with wildlife watching is universal. Nature is "the real thing." Man was clever enough to create tools, to erect magnificent skyscrapers of architectural beauty, and to build millions of "horseless carriages" that dash over the network of asphalt ribbons covering the land. The age of technology has given man a longer life with less toil and greater comfort than kings of old dreamed of. But there has been a price. In fewer than two hundred years, millions of acres of America have been razed, as a burgeoning population, long-lived because of improved health conditions, has required space to grow.

In many areas, the air is no longer sweet. The natural music of nature is drowned in a cacophony created by men at work and at play. We accomplish more in less time, but swift change has brought what one author has called "future shock." There has been a divorce between environment and self. No one is suggesting a leap back to a time without space-age machines and vaccinations, but I am suggesting that man and his natural environment need to be reconciled. A better understanding of nature promotes a better understanding of ourselves and helps us to live rich and rewarding lives in our busy technosociety.

We are becoming more aware. We work hard, and we're also learning to live better, recognizing that the physical and mental are linked. Good health is promoted; diet plans and exercise programs abound. And we are urged to take a dose of the outdoors as part of our health plan. The natural excitement of wildlife watching has become a tonic for many of us who spend much of our time behind desks.

Why watch wildlife? Because it is a re-

Fascination with wildlife is natural for man. Generally, we learn our fears from example. Nicole Fadala examines a bullsnake before releasing it back into its environment.

As civilization advances, with roads and housing developments, wildlife niches change, but they are not necessarily destroyed. Above this city, there remain large parcels of land that can be enjoyed by the wildlife watcher.

Wildlife watching brings its own reward. Here, John Fadala waits for a great horned owl to emerge from its shelter.

Involvement in nature uplifts the spirit. It is difficult to harbor stressful feelings when enjoying a view such as this one.

warding leisure activity that improves our outlook as well as our understanding. Honing our natural senses to a new level of awareness brings self-confidence. Isolation from nature diminishes us; involvement in nature uplifts the spirit. Tension is relieved. The subconscious mind is fed calming information, which results in a positive mindset. Wildlife watching is therapy, and nature is the therapist.

Using This Book

The projects in this book are designed to increase your enjoyment and proficiency in wildlife watching. Each project follows a thread of continuity. First there is an *introduction,* providing a justification for the project; then the *object,* relating its value. You will learn what *equipment* is needed, equipment that is modest in scope and cost. *Methods and procedures,* the heart of the project, are discussed. *Recordable observations,* the results of the project, are outlined. And finally, a *conclusion* is drawn for each project.

1

Project Wildwatch Diary

INTRODUCTION

Serious wildlife watchers will want to record their findings. Bits of random information often fit together like a puzzle, with each observation connecting to another to form a clear picture. There can be a great deal of pleasure in keeping a journal of what you see.

Because most of us are interested in the life around us, we need no notes to remember the major events that take place in our wildlife watching. Our photographs, movies, videos, and recording tapes freeze what we see and hear for future reliving.

We don't, however, always recall the fine details unless we record them. We are in good company when we keep records. Charles Darwin, for example, was a naturalist, not a laboratory researcher. He observed wildlife in its natural setting with meticulous care, and his observations became books. Our observations may not become books, but they still may be very important.

Our notebooks can be a legacy to others. My second son, John, has been keeping a wildlife notebook for years. Someday a son or daughter of his may find John's notes and observations very interesting. So our wildwatch diaries can be important to ourselves, and perhaps to our protégés of the future.

Notes taken in the past have often proved very valuable to present-day nature lovers. For example, when I was living in Patagonia, Arizona, an older resident who kept an almanac of the region told me that a great change in the water table had taken place over the years. His records were clear, and I passed this information on to a biologist who compared wildlife

We may observe patterns that can be recorded. These young prairie dogs act and interact in specific ways. By keeping a record of these traits, a biological story may emerge.

trends with water availability. The written observations of that pioneer helped to shed light on several important scientific ecological questions.

We may observe *patterns,* but if we do not make notes of these patterns, it becomes very difficult, even impossible, to map and detail future changes with accuracy. A wildlife watcher observed a decrease in white-winged doves over a period of ten years. He began to ask questions, and he found answers. Nesting sites near his home had been slowly but constantly eroded. His backyard wildlife niche was not large enough to make a difference in white-winged population, although he did have nesting birds on his property. The white-winged dove's major "nurseries" had dwindled. The trees had been re-

moved, and with them had fallen the overall population of birds in that region.

We may also note *connections.* There are often connections between events in nature; one episode leads to another in a cause-and-effect sequence. My wife and I had a very interesting and highly populated wildlife garden when we lived in the Southwest. There were several long-eared desert jackrabbits that came daily to drink in our cement water hole, which we replenished on a regular basis. Then the rabbit visits ceased.

For a period of two weeks our journal showed not one sighting of a jackrabbit at the water hole. I "dusted" the area, that is, I swept all around the watering hole with a broom. The dusting served to prove further that the rabbits were no longer coming to our water tank, as such sites are called on the desert.

One evening I was observing the area from my porch. My binoculars brought an interesting sight to my eyes. A pack of coyotes was working the area systematically, back and forth, combing the underbrush. Normally, packs of coyotes amount to a couple of animals, which often set up such an intense evening serenade that they sound like a dozen desert dogs or more. This, however, was a pack of seven animals ranging together. We found their prints at our water hole often in the next few weeks, and then the coyotes moved on. I'm not sure why they gave up on a territory that seemed to be well established, but their tracks were no longer found in the dust by the cement water hole, and their nightly songs were no longer heard. We were sad to see them go, but when they did, the jacks came back. This is an example of a probable connection.

Your diary may note *trends* as well. An interesting example of microevolution took place in London during the industrial revolution. Observers noticed that the white moths that frequented the area were growing darker. Coal dust had darkened the buildings, making the white moths ever more visible to birds, which were decimating the moth population. The moths *adapted* to the situation by growing darker. Simple observation proved this to be true, offering proof that, although our wildlife diaries are for our personal enlightenment and pleasure, they may also serve in other capacities.

OBJECT OF THE PROJECT

The object of the wildwatch diary is to create a record by building a word story

of your observations. I have a record of a nearby population of ground squirrels that is showing a sharp downward cycling trend. Perhaps the small rodents have reached a peak at which their habitat is saturated. Although it seems that the population has room for expansion, there has been no attempt at building burrows away from their original niche. Where once literally hundreds of squirrels could be seen going about their business, none have been seen recently. Why have the squirrels vanished? Predators? Unlikely. This is another wildlife mystery that intrigues me.

A wildlife diary can improve wildwatch methods. Finding out what does not work often leads to better ways of watching, and a clear, detailed set of notes helps to build a story about methods and success.

EQUIPMENT

You need little equipment for a wildlife diary or notebook. I prefer a loose-leaf ledger. Spiral notebooks don't work when you want to insert new information. Even when you keep separate notebooks on each species, the spiral notebook precludes adding or updating information.

A recipe file with notecards is workable. It can be segregated with dividers for various species, and notecards can be added to each category as it develops.

A regular diary can also be used for wildlife watching, but using a diary changes the method of entering data and makes locating a given species or event considerably more difficult than the loose-leaf or recipe file approach. However, you may prefer this more informal manner of keeping a notebook. Because you add to the diary on a regular basis as you make observations, the day-by-day diary can be more fun to read than the loose-leaf notebook. There is something personal about this sort of ledger; the loose-leaf or file methods tend to render the observer more scientific in his entries.

METHODS AND PROCEDURES

I write in ink. Pencil is fine but may tend to smear. I prefer a fine-point pen for neat, cursive writing or printing.

I make my notes in pencil on notepaper, then transfer them in ink to a file. They tend to fall between the informal and the scientific. I recommend this approach, but I certainly don't insist on it. Here is a very

One kind of wildwatch diary is a recipe file such as this one. The loose cards offer an advantage in organization and updating of data.

In evening camp, the author goes over his daily notes, which will later be transferred to a card file.

short example of an entry card for a horned lizard.

Entry 212
Horned Lizard
July 26, 1986

Eighty miles west of Casper, Wyoming, elevation 7,000 feet above sea level. Warm day. Only temperature reading taken was at 11:00 A.M., showing 87 degrees F. No wind. Dry.

The horned lizard, I noticed, was unlike his cousins that lived east of the area. It had an array of white spots on its back, which I've never seen on other horned lizards in Wyoming. I was eating my lunch and watching my subject at the same time. The lizard remained motionless, on a rock, in the shade of a bush for about fifteen minutes. Then it climbed the rock to a higher elevation. I did not see the insect (could not determine for sure, but probably a small grasshopper) in the bush, but I noted tail movement and a lunge forward and the lizard had a meal. There was no sound that my ears could pick up. The body language of the lizard indicated "excitement" with tail movement. Its eye movement was interesting because the head remained still as the eyes seemed to scan about.

It ignored me completely; however, I was very still, making no sudden movements. I was only a foot away from the horned lizard as it crawled down the rock, stopping in the sunlight for about a minute, and then making it back into the shade. A hawk flew overhead and circled. The lizard made no movement and gave no indication of notice. The lizard left the rock finally and disappeared into the bush.

Not a very exciting entry, but a realistic one. The horned lizard episode was valuable to me because from it I learned that there was a variety of horned lizard in the area that was different from all of the others I had seen earlier. I noted the white spots on two more horned lizards that day. These horned lizards displayed several traits unique among their kind: the sedentary nature; tail movement indicating action to come; avoidance of the direct sunlight for a long period of time; scanning eye movement; relatively slow speed compared with other lizards, and yet very swift and precise action in capturing prey, all in quietness, with no sound emitted that a person would normally hear—in short, the traits associated with the horned lizard were revealed in this little observation, and I had found a type of horned lizard I'd never seen before.

Here is what one of my correspondents wrote in his daily wildlife diary.

I listened to the rain beating on the tin roof of the shed all night long, but the old roof held up and my sleeping bag never did get wet. When I woke up in the morning, fog filled the valley. I couldn't see ten feet from the portal of the shed. I got a fire started and was pleased to learn that there was no precipitation with the fog. Soon, the sun burned through, and what could have been a dismal day turned out to be bright and sunny, with big white clouds in the sky. I was trying a new call that I had bought, seeing if I could get one of those handsome Ohio farm whitetailed deer out of the trees and into the open. My camera was set up on a tripod, and I had a bulb attached to release the shutter.

The Twin Tube call was brand-new to me, but it wasn't difficult to master. In ten minutes I had a whitetail buck in my frame. He was a beauty. His neck was thick with the rut and his late fall coat was sleek. I had the motor drive on. I figured that it would be worth the clack-clack of the motor if I could get a series of pictures with the buck coming head-on, then bolting away. But he didn't bolt away. He stopped. And he looked right into the camera lens, and the sun glinted from his eyes. He gave me the best whitetail pictures I've yet obtained.

The tone of the entry above is personal and nonscientific with the observer's feel-

Wildlife watchers take note of animal behavior. This fawn antelope is using a low profile to remain out of danger. Even its ears are flat!

ings included. The wildlife watcher went on to describe several factors concerning his outing, including the location of various scrapes, and a fight between two whitetailed buck deer that he could hear but couldn't see. He made notes of tracks and rubs and added personal comments along the way.

"Equipment" used by the observer was, obviously, his eyes and his ears. The human nose, as we shall see later, sometimes plays a role in gathering nuances of information from the environment. You can also use cameras and tape recorders to freeze wildlife memories forever.

RECORDABLE OBSERVATIONS

The above short samples contain only a shred of the possible recordable observations with which a wildlife notebook may be filled; there are many others.

Wildlife watching falls into the realm of science called ethology. Ethology deals with wild creatures in their natural habitat rather than under prepared conditions. It is the study of animal behavior—primarily, a biology of behavior, for it includes not only how the animal acts, but also how it *reacts* to its environment. Konrad Lorenz is credited as one of the founding fathers of ethology. For his work in ethology, he was awarded the Nobel Prize in physiology and medicine in 1973, along with Tinbergen and von Frisch.

Our wildlife watching is also mainly, but not always, in the natural setting. My basement window burrow is an example of studying animals in a prepared habitat; so is watching wildlife around a bird feeder or squirrel house. None of these, however, is the same as a laboratory setting. Wild animals react very differently under true laboratory conditions. Even the ferocious shark can become docile and meek when enclosed in a small tank; some have had to be hand fed even when there were plenty of fish in the tank for food.

Most wildwatch observations fall into the realm of the fixed action pattern, the movements or postures of wildlife that communicate their intentions, such as curiosity, flight and fight syndromes, threat, conflict, fear, and even decision-making in wild animals. Konrad Lorenz is credited as a pioneer in recording fixed action patterns.

Of course, it's always a temptation to fall into the anthropomorphic trap. Anthropomorphic means attributing our own characteristics and emotions to animals. For example, when I stated in my entry that the horned lizard exhibited excitement in his body language, I was humanizing the lizard. Something other than the human emotion of excitement may have caused the tail wag.

I was on a high ridge one spring day using a deer call, which was working better than the Pied Piper's flute. Mostly female deer were answering the call. They would come in "bristled up" as if ready to fight. Was the emotion anger? Or belligerence? Or something else altogether? I can't say; no one can for sure. But in my log I entered "deer came into the call with a belligerent attitude toward the sound."

On the one hand, it's dangerous to make such statements, but on the other hand we must work from our own platform; therefore, we tend to use human terms to describe animal actions. Such descriptions make sense to others. I am sure that you can visualize the deer coming into the call, bristled and bothered, stamping their feet and looking for the source of their disturbance.

Another time I sat in the mountains watching a trail through binoculars. I slowly digested the scene as a whitetailed buck (Coues deer) climbed to higher terrain. He came to a fork in the trail and stopped. He looked right; he looked left. Then he turned to his right and ambled upward. Did he not make a *decision?* I think so. We have all seen animals making choices on one level or another; however, any conclusions we make about those choices remain on shaky grounds. Did your dog decide on dog biscuit A instead of dog biscuit B when you offered them to him, or did he react to one aroma totally from instinct? Who can say for sure?

We judge from the human standpoint. We have no other standards that we understand nearly so well. So when you enter that the animal "looked angry," that may be less than scientific, but it's not necessarily a poor comment. When watching an animal's ears, you may give anthropomorphic accounts of what the animal does with those ears. We know from watching our pet dogs that the position of the ears can tell us a great deal about the animal's disposition, from being "embarrassed" about being scolded, to angry and perhaps even prepared to attack as a strange dog invades the home territory.

We also must be careful about drawing

conclusions too quickly. Had Jane Goodall stopped looking at chimp behavior after a few months, or even a few years, she never would have discovered their penchant for eating meat, for example, or for hunting smaller animals for food.

Making observations at different times of day and seasons and including the time and season in your notes is important, for animals react very differently to each other and to their world at different times. The American pronghorn antelope, for example, is certainly a different creature during the "rut" than during the rest of the year. The male may become bellicose, driving other males away, even entering into skirmishes to protect a harem of does. He is now putting to flight the very same bucks he was "pals" with earlier when they may have been living in a bachelor herd of all male animals.

There are other things that need to be noted, as well, because of their influence on animal behavior. Temperatures make a difference. A rattlesnake encountered on a cold morning is one thing; the same snake on a warm afternoon can be quite another. I also like to note the locale because of territorial divisions. My horned lizard was certainly not the same creature I had been seeing in another area. Condition of the animal is another important factor. I

A rattlesnake on a cold morning is lethargic. By keeping notes, wildlife watchers learn of behavioral patterns.

rescued a trapped sparrow hawk from a fence line where its leg had been badly broken when caught on a barb. The bird displayed hostility at first, and then total docility, not even attempting to fly when held in the flat of my hand. Certainly, the condition of the bird precipitated its behavior.

Animal sounds are very hard to record in writing, so I've turned to the tape recorder when possible. I was in Baja several years ago when the whales were coming through. At that time, "whale songs" were not considered as profound as some consider them today. They just sounded interesting to people. I attempted to make notes of these sounds, but as I look back I realize that the notes were entirely inadequate; I should have used a tape recorder.

We can make certain remarks about sounds that give a clue—loud, soft, screech, grunt, growl; but there are many animal sounds that defy description and others that we can't even hear. Recording instruments can make us aware that these sounds are present but outside of the human range.

The howl of coyotes got me up one night as I camped on the Arizona-Mexico border. When I say the noises were "hair-raising," I do so for lack of a better descriptive term. The next morning I walked into the area from which the howling had come and found what was left of a doe. The fresh remains of the deer, the many coyote tracks, and the condition of the dead animal led me to believe that the sounds I had heard the night before were those of coyotes in the full frenzy of hunting. While it's impossible to relate the exact sounds I heard with the written word, I believe the notes were worthwhile because the reader can relate to "howling" and to "hair-raising."

Notes concerning whale music, for example, led scientists to further study the tremendously complicated patterns of sound. Researchers learned that some whale songs lasted thirty minutes and conveyed many messages that are still a mystery and may remain so until much more study reveals their meaning.

We have learned that the sweet songs of birds often denote a territorial announcement and proclamation—"I live here and if you enter, be ready to pay the price." By recording wild creature sounds, we can sometimes put a story of communication together.

One night in a small abandoned shack in the mountains I was awakened by a "thump, thump, thump" coming from inside the little room, but I could not pinpoint it at first. I lighted the gas lantern and looked around. Finally, in some rubble, I found a woodrat entrapped with a coil of fine wire wrapped around its leg. Two other woodrats were by the victim's side. Had they been called by a help signal? I'm not sure, but after observing wild animals for about 40 years, I wouldn't be surprised at such a communication. The timid woodrats did not flee as I unchained their companion. Then the three rodents disappeared through a hole in the wooden floor. The only other time I heard the thumping sound was under nearly identical circumstances; a woodrat captured when he decided to drop into a kettle he couldn't climb back out of.

CONCLUSION

Your notebook can be just about anything you want it to be, from a very careful and scientific record of everything from humidity to body language to a simple record of basic observations. Either way, the notebook is of value because it sets down events and conditions that simply won't be remembered in detail otherwise.

We observe the animal's reaction to other animals of its own or a different species; its reaction to the weather, from bright sunlight to pouring rain; the temperature; the exact ecological niche; its fixed action pattern; and its response to many stimuli. It's our task to observe the entire organism. Ethology is not a dissection; no observation should be considered in isolation. Even when we are noting a wild animal's reaction and learned behavior to a man-made setting, such as our wildlife gardens, we need to integrate that information with what we have learned from other settings.

Finally, don't forget the child. Children's wildlife notebooks can be very enlightening, and don't be surprised when their observations surpass your own. They haven't yet learned to see things a certain set way, the "right" way, so they see things their way, which can be most interesting.

A wildlife notebook can be an excellent means of helping a youngster develop his writing talents as well as his ability to observe events and carefully note details. Children have a tendency to humanize animals, but in many respects, that fact aids communication. The young person learns to transmit ideas in a language understood by all, with metaphors that relate to human emotions and expressions.

But before you can record any informa-

Observation is so important to wildlife understanding that the professionals sometimes mark an animal for study. This mother antelope wears a collar with a number. Its patterns of movement within the environment will be recorded.

tion about wildlife watching, you have to find and observe wildlife. Much of the rest of this book is dedicated to that search. In the next chapter, you'll learn how to sharpen your vision and see more of the environment around you, that part that for now goes unnoticed. And if you wish to keep a memory book of your findings rather than a highly structured ledger, do so. Your personal wildlife notebook may become a more important project than you think.

2

Project Sharp Vision

INTRODUCTION

A sliver of moon ignited a patch of eastern sky over the mountain range. Flanked by two stars, it rested above an ever-reddening glow on the horizon. The rising sun seemed to be pushing the moon and its partners out of the heavens. They grew ever fainter.

Morning sounds came from the creek bottom as I slid into my parka. With my 10x50 B&L binoculars on a padded strap around my neck, I walked to the top of the rise. Technically it was still late summer, but there was a fall chill in the air. I lifted the hood on the parka, wedged myself against a fallen pine tree, and scanned the vast arena before me. The image through the binoculars was bright and sharp. In only a few minutes I saw a golden eagle, several deer, one coyote, and the animal I wanted to photograph. Many of them, in fact.

The territory was transitory in nature. I sat amidst the pine trees that dominated up-mountain behind me. Below, the plains rolled away in a golden early-morning undulation of grasses. Antelope herds punctuated the open expanse.

I paced downhill to camp and pulled my partner away from our small campfire. "Get your Brownie out," I said. "You wanted antelope photos for your wildlife album, and there are several herds down below us." He slipped three 35mm cameras around his neck, along with several lenses, and we began walking downhill. "There's a nice herd at the mouth of that draw," I told him.

He trained his binoculars on the spot. "I don't see it."

"Right there. Look at that last tree on the ridge. Then look left of it. The herd is standing in the open."

"I see the tree, but I don't see the antelope."

"You can't miss them. There are at least 15 animals in plain sight in the grassy part of the draw."

"I only see some orange-looking things, but . . . wait. They moved. Oh, right. I see them now."

What were plainly antelope to me were "some orange things" to my friend before he made those orange things out to be what they were—a whole herd of antelope. It seemed remarkable that anyone could look at that herd in the golden light of morning and not recognize it instantly as a bunch of pronghorns. However, I knew what antelope looked like in an aura of early morning sun piercing the high country atmosphere. My friend probably could have spotted the prairie goats quickly if they had been animals that resided in his region because he's one of the best wildlife photographers around.

That story exemplifies the importance of this chapter. No matter how sharp your vision is, if you don't know what to look for outdoors, or how to look for it, you may see right through or past some of the most interesting wildlife.

OBJECT OF THE PROJECT

This chapter is about how you can visually locate and enjoy wild creatures that often go entirely unnoticed. The person who sharpens his outdoor vision will benefit immeasurably. Imagine a gray movie screen with blank celluloid projected on it. You hear the projector whirring away, but you see nothing except a gray flicker. Contrast that picture with a

From a distance, the cream-colored rump patches of these mule deer will identify them, provided the wildwatcher knows what to look for.

long look at a feeding deer, its image reflected in a pond, or a raccoon making its way to his den in early morning, or the simple sight of birds flitting through the high trees, or a scolding squirrel in the local park.

The object of this project is to improve wildlife sightings. Sometimes it's easy to catch sight of animals and birds going about their business; no special talent or knowledge is required to spot an elk in Yellowstone Park as it feeds in the open— although even this huge animal could blend into his environment, requiring wildlife-sighting know-how.

But quite often we miss the unfolding of the wildlife drama before us because we are visually oblivious to it. We are oblivious because we are trained *not to see* much of our normal and usual environment. Why train your eyes to see your neighborhood, the bus on the street, the tall buildings, the sidewalk? I find little interest in the fine points along the way from my home to the post office—except in winter when the deer have moved down-mountain and I can watch them feeding along the creek bottoms on the way to town. We are not taught as children to observe our natural world closely, so we have learned *not* to observe.

A parent or teacher must expend conscious effort to show a child *how* to look at his surroundings. "Look at that hummingbird. See how it hovers at the flower? Now watch the long bill. What do you think the bird is doing with that long beak poked into the flower?" We can scratch the surface of any person's powers of observation by asking questions.

Since it is not usually part of modern child rearing to sharpen the powers of observation, we may have to improve those talents as adults. Was wildlife-watching part of your training? It wasn't part of mine. We *learn* to become sensitive to our surroundings, and it is the object of this chapter to advance that learning. Truly seeing the landscape within our view means becoming visually sensitive to *everything* in our scope. We will never achieve a perfect level of visual awareness, but we can become far better observers through conscious effort.

EQUIPMENT

Very little equipment is needed for this multifaceted project. Binoculars are es-sential. They need not be expensive. True, high-priced binoculars offer better optical definition and longer life. The better built glass is often more accurately colli-mated—that is, the barrels, and therefore the lenses, are correctly positioned so there is very little eye fatigue when using the binocular for a long period of time. Top-grade binoculars stay in collimation despite moderate abuse; cheaper glasses tend to go astray if they are knocked about.

The wildlife watcher is, however, very fortunate today, because optical technol-ogy has produced many excellent models at very modest cost. Furthermore, a large number of fine used binoculars are for sale. Even better ones do not have a high resale value. You can often buy a beautiful pair of previously owned glasses for a small price; try garage sales.

Optical excellence—what is it? For our purposes, the binocular that exhibits opti-cal excellence has high definition (optical resolution). We need to know how to test our own binoculars in order to determine how well they will resolve the things we wish to bring closer to us. There are many ways. For years, I have used a very simple, but workable, method of separating bet-ter binoculars from the also-rans. This method can work for you, too.

My "test" consists of two parts. My front porch looks out upon a distant scene of open ranchland with a lonely road winding its way through it. On that road, probably two miles away, there is a metal object. It appears to have been red and white once; now it is red, white, and rusty. For years I've taken test binoculars to the porch for a look at my mystery object.

The mystery object was so named be-cause the first binoculars used to observe it revealed nothing more than a "blob."

Optical excellence aids the wildlife watcher in his quest for interesting creatures to study. These Bausch & Lomb 10x50 binoculars are exemplary of high definition and top lens quality.

Binoculars of better optical quality defined the object as a piece of twisted metal. For some time, the "test" object's identity remained unknown. Then two pairs of high-quality binoculars arrived for testing, an 8x42 and a 10x50. The mystery object was immediately identified through these binoculars. It was a car fender. Even in the low light of late afternoon, the light-gathering 10x50 glass was able to define the distant test object (due to the binocular's large objective lens and high magnification). This is an illustration of excellent optical resolution, a characteristic of high-grade binoculars.

My second means of testing binoculars is also very simple—I read signs with them. Testing binoculars before buying is sometimes difficult, especially in a store. Every binocular may look great, since nothing you look at is far away, and the area is well lighted. So walk to a window

and look down the street. Avoiding the bright neons, try reading the more distant signs. It's not scientific, but you may be surprised at the results. There can be remarkable differences in the optical ability of each glass to define distant lettering.

After optical excellence, consider construction of the glass. The high-grade binocular is well-made. Through internal design and strong materials, the lenses tend to remain properly aligned. The barrels of a well-made binocular stay in collimation. High quality binoculars, which exhibit optical excellence *and* top-grade construction, are expensive. The wildwatcher, however, can get by with modestly priced binoculars if he recognizes that the less expensive glass must be handled carefully, with even greater care than the higher quality unit. The less costly glass will not stand up to the abuse of bounces or drops.

The next criteria to look for are magnification and diameter of objective lenses. Close-focus ability also is important if any of your study objects will be at close

Sign-reading with binoculars is a viable means of determining optical excellence without the use of special equipment

range — hummingbirds at a feeder, for example. Close-focus binoculars can be very useful in the wildlife garden, park, or wildlife refuge where birds and animals allow people to get very close to them.

Magnification. Which optical strength is best for the modern wildlife watcher? The tried and trusted 7X (seven-power) binocular is always a good choice. Glasses with more power magnify the interesting wild creature in your view, but they are also harder to hold. Your natural body tremor or "shake" may obscure the image. Practiced wildlife watchers can hand-hold glasses of greater than 7X, to be sure. The rule of thumb says that a steady hand can master up to 9X magnification. But that varies with the individual and with experience. I use a pair of 10X glasses that, partially due to their comparatively high mass, are rather easily steadied. So the 7X rule is relative. It may or may not apply to you.

Try binoculars of different power. If you can hold greater than 7X magnification without having a blurred picture from body tremor, then by all means consider the greater power. Naturally, the object of your interest is going to be brought closer, and you are going to see more detail with the higher power instrument. I have three binoculars I use a great deal; a compact 7X, an 8X, and a 10X. If I had to throw two of the three away, I'd be forced to stay with the middle glass — medium power, medium weight, medium size.

But the power number is not the only figure that describes a binocular. The unit may be, for example, a 7x24. I have such a glass. It is seven-power and it has an objective lens — the lens away from the eye — that is 24mm in size. That's small. These glasses are of exceptional optical quality and construction; therefore, they show me

a lot. When the light of day wanes, however, a larger objective lens pays off. The common 7x35 is still the industry standard — seven-power with an objective lens 35mm across.

You may have a 7x50, seven-power again, but with an objective lens a full 50mm across. And there are even larger objective lenses. For our purposes it's all right to think of binoculars with large objective lenses as gathering more light than do binoculars with smaller objective lenses.

But there's a price. My fine 10x50 glass offers a comparatively bright late afternoon and early evening picture, but it weighs plenty. No compact, these binoculars. The little 7x24s weigh only sixteen ounces and my 8x42s, twenty-eight ounces, but my 10x50s weigh forty-six ounces. Size of glass can make a significant effect upon user enjoyment. If you don't want to carry the larger instrument, the compact is the wise choice. It will not, generally, do quite the work of the heavier glass of the same class and cost, but it will show you many wonderful magnified scenes. Only if you need the greater light-gathering ability of the heavier tool should you select the large objective models.

One dimly lighted afternoon, I was driving home through a high mountain pass when a large black object caught my eye way below along the river. There was a handy pullover spot, so I drifted to the side of the road. I had two pairs of binoculars with me, 7x35 and 7x50. I'd been using the former when hiking and the latter while driving along old logging roads in the forest. The 7x35s showed me clearly that the distant black form in the trees was a large animal. I knew it had to be a moose, but the 7x35 glass couldn't prove it. The image was not bright enough in that dull light. Then I lifted my 7x50s, and instantly the blob in the trees grew a set of antlers. It was a moose all right, a big moose. But I wouldn't have enjoyed that wildlife experience without the light-gathering ability of the large-objective (but heavy) glass.

Close-focus. So many wonderful wildlife observations take place in the backyard or at the nearby park at abbreviated distances that a glass that will not close-focus is a real detriment. Be certain that your prospective wildlife binocular focuses close enough for your needs. I have owned glasses that showed nearby wildlife, such as birds on the feeder, as no more than a blur because they would not focus down to a few yards. No matter the quality, no matter the light-gathering ability of the optical tool, all is for naught if the cardinal at your birdhouse can't be enjoyed in a clear, magnified view. Study the literature with your binocular before you buy. Be certain that the tool will focus close enough to suit your personal wild-watching conditions.

Field of view. This is the width encompassed optically in the binocular at 1,000 yards. Therefore, we say that a binocular has a field of view of so many feet at 1,000 yards. For example, the B&L 7x35 Classic's field of view is 446 feet at 1,000 yards. The B&L 7x35 Explorer has a field of view of 419 feet at 1,000 yards. The same company offers an extra-wide-angle 7x35 glass with a field of view of 576 feet at 1,000 yards.

Never select a binocular based upon field of view as the major criterion, however. If you prefer a glass that magnifies a large area, fine. But I consider field of view less important than optical resolution, construction of the instrument, fo-

cusing distance, and price. I have found the standard field of view large enough for my personal wildlife viewing.

Selection of the binocular is very important to any wildlife watcher, and that's why Project Sharp Vision has included this extensive look at the field glass. It boils down to buying the binocular right for you; right in size and weight, focusing distance, power, optical quality, and price.

Today, the problem of finding the right glass is much reduced compared with ten or twenty years ago, when an inexpensive binocular was usually very poor in quality. Today you need not spend much money to buy a good glass.

A glass does much more than magnify the world of wild creatures. Yes, it brings wildlife into your lap, so to speak, but it also allows much more precise observation of wildlife *behavior.* The binocular makes wildlife watching more interesting and isolates the specific ecological niche of a species. You can't do without it.

Another tool that is valuable in wildlife watching is the terrestrial telescope. Today there are very good compact "spotting scopes" available to the wildlife watcher, and most of them have variable eyepieces. My own model is 10X-30X. At 10X there is sufficient field of view to locate distant wildlife; at 30X, there is sufficient magnification to bring the subject into your lap.

A little scope set up in your backyard can show close wildlife in amazing detail. I once had a wildlife garden in the Southwest with a panorama that stretched from my porch for several hundred yards. Many wild creatures were drawn close with a telescope and were studied in whisker-by-whisker detail through the high magnification of the scope. The hiker will appreciate the compact scope and a lightweight tripod; the nonhiker may prefer the standard model. Either way, a terrestrial tele-scope can add a lot to wildlife watching because of its high magnification.

Eyeglasses or contact lenses may be vital. Don't shortchange yourself. The most important "tool" in wildlife watch-ing is your eyesight. Get a visual checkup, and buy corrective lenses if your eyes need them. Make a habit of having periodic checkups to ensure that your glasses or contacts are still correct for your particu-lar visual problem.

METHODS AND PROCEDURES

This multifaceted project is one of the more important of the book. After all, you have to sight wildlife before you can enjoy it. What makes wildlife so difficult to see? Wild animals often remain mo-tionless, or nearly so, for hours at a time. Many animals are active at night, seden-tary during the day. They may be camou-flaged, not only through coloration, but also because of their habitat. Birds in a backyard tree are not always easy to spot when they mingle among the leaves, for example, even when they are only a few yards away. Wildlife often fits into its niche. If you are hoping to see a bird or animal standing out from its background, you will usually be disappointed.

If wildlife is so often difficult to see, then why are there so many successful birdwatchers and other enthusiasts who not only locate wild creatures but also ac-tually get close enough to photograph them down to an eyelash? The answer lies in training and experience. As alluded to earlier, we can learn better binocular tech-nique by studying with a knowledgeable partner. That learning is further enhanced through experience, which helps us im-prove our technique. Watch wildlife often

in your own backyard, nearby park or on outings. You will become more proficient with each added experience. I will be sug-gesting ways of improving outdoor vision, but first think in terms of gaining more outdoor observation experience, even in your backyard. Each time you attempt to locate a wild creature, you make another deposit in your bank of wildlife-finding ability.

I was walking through a sagebrush area of rolling hills, 35mm camera slung over a shoulder, when something told me to stop and look more closely at a bush I had just glanced at. We are not always aware of what we see at first glance, and such was the case here. I looked at the bush again and saw nothing unusual. Then I saw it. There *was* something different about this bush after all. The head of a rattlesnake was growing out of it! Camouflage is not a strong enough term to describe how that head melded and blended into the leaf pattern of the bush. It would have been invisible to me at one time, but years of visual training backed by experience showed me what I would not have seen otherwise.

I took a photo, which was like trying to capture on film a black cat in an unlighted coal mine shaft. The snake blended so well with its sagebrush habitat that when the photo was developed, I had to mark the head of the serpent with an arrow.

The trained eye learns to *interpret* cor-rectly the optical message brought through it to the brain. My eye had ob-served a bush, no more. But it had also collected another image in the bush, the head of the snake. The brain did not at first perceive and identify that image.

There are many methods of improving wildwatch vision. Learn to observe *sys-tematically*. Try this—your local park or

Camouflaged in the bush was a rattlesnake. Because of its sedentary nature and coloration, this snake is almost invisible to the human observer.

backyard is a good place for this basic project. Look first for the overt or "big picture." *Use your peripheral vision, rather than tunnel vision.* Study the whole scene. Now, where would you concentrate if you were looking for a specific wild creature?

Narrow your field of vision. Perhaps your interest lies in observing a tree squirrel. After a general scan of the area, concentrate your view on the floor of the woods, where squirrels often dash about at their business, and then into the trees where they spend much of their time. The pattern is general view to specific view.

Newcomers to wildlife watching often spend too much of their time looking for a creature where that creature will never

(or seldom) be. First, practice the "big picture" by gaining a panoramic view of the territory before you. Then isolate each segment of that panorama, intensifying your visual search upon those specific niches normally occupied by your subject. Simple? Of course. But observers quite often fail to focus their attention area by area.

If isolating an area visually is difficult for you at first, try the "owl eye." Simply curl your forefinger and thumb of both hands into a small circle. Overlap the other six fingers of your two hands to make a "roof" or shade. Then place the circles of thumb and forefinger right into the orbits of your eyes like binoculars.

This results in cutting down the super-

The use of the "owl eye" method of observation cuts out superfluous light and concentrates the vision to a specific area.

fluous light around the eye and in isolating the area before you. It's good practice to learn first to focus on the large picture and then to isolate sections of that view for a closer and more specific look. You may also close one hand into a loose fist, leaving a passageway in the center. Looking through that will help isolate the view. Binoculars will later do the same thing, blocking out all but the area of magnification for your study. But learn first to look into specific areas of the environment by using the owl eye or loose fist approach to focus your vision.

In that little picture, search for motion. Hone your awareness of movement — the flick of a bird wing, the switch of a tail. You can *learn* to see these things much better than you see them now. Become sensitive to motion. Again, take the big picture into view, then force yourself to visually isolate each part of it. Look first for motion in each segment. Your alertness to such motion will become more sensitive as you practice. Experience soon plays a major role in this exercise, because you will learn to *identify* each motion.

You will instantly know the blur of a squirrel moving from limb to limb as it differs from the flutter of a bird wing in the same ecological niche. Practice identifying each motion.

Look for the part, not the whole. It is vital to reverse your point of view. Think in terms of being the wildlife for a moment, and remember why wild creatures are so often difficult to spot. Think of being bedded down in a thicket. What shows? A whole animal? No, only a part of an animal. Think of the bird in the tree. What shows? A whole bird? Sometimes, but usually not. More often only part of the bird is clearly visible among the leaves and branches. So practice looking for the part, not the whole, and learn to make meaning of that part.

Remain mentally alert, and when you tire, rest. I was looking for whales in Baja California. You would think that anyone could spot a whale at any time. However, this was a matter of viewing a vast section of salt water from a desert cliff. After an hour of watching whitecaps, I caught myself looking at the water, not looking for whales. In fact, my ear brought the message of whales to me before my eyes did. It's very easy to become lulled into a visual trance when observing in the outdoors, even in your own wildlife garden. It's often calming and pleasant, which is just what we want; however, we still have to remain mentally alert in order to identify the images being scanned by the eye and interpreted by the brain.

Achieve *perspective*. You can practice this, too. Learn the visual size of things as they exist in their environment. I was with a newcomer to wildlife watching in Yellowstone Park. "Look," my friend said, "a bear!" Across a grassy meadow, there was an animal moving about slowly. Before I

Look for a part, not the whole animal. This rabbit was located by the light shining through its pink ears as it nestled in the brush.

raised my glass, I knew that this was no bear. In fact, the object of our attention was not as large as a dog. My friend had lost all perspective. What to him was a bear in a distant meadow was in fact a porcupine fewer than 100 yards away.

Another time, I mistook a 6,000-pound boulder for an elk in much the same setting. The boulder was shaped like an elk and as tall as some of the smaller jack pines around it. Learn perspective through conscious effort by being aware of the size of things in the environment,

such as trees and boulders. Then experience will take over and you will unconsciously learn to size things up outdoors.

And now the most important part of our project—using the binocular correctly. The simplest use of the binocular is to get a magnified look at what you have already seen. You see a bird, raise the binoculars to your eyes, and enhance the view with magnification. In your own backyard or at the local park, along the river in birdwatching, anywhere you can enjoy wildlife watching, you can practice with the binocular in this way. Look at an object, try to identify it, and *then* put the glass up to verify your conclusion. Thus you will improve your general wild-watching ability. You will learn to identify those natural optical illusions that exist so frequently in the outdoors.

But that's not all there is to it. You can also learn to *find wildlife with the binocular*, and I mean wildlife that may be a mile or more away — feeding, even bedded down, lying prone along a limb of a tree, curled up by a rock, nestled in a thicket. This sort of finding requires practice, of course, but it also demands a method. You can't merely peer through your glass and expect to find wild creatures immediately.

First, get steady. *You* get steady. Forget about the glass. Ensure that your body is comfortable. If you are too cool, put your jacket on. Prepare yourself so that your body is under control. This may mean sitting comfortably, perhaps with your back supported against a tree or smooth boulder.

Second, steady your binocular. I use a

Using a walking staff to steady a binocular makes it easier to distinguish wildlife.

walking staff with a padded top for hiking, and when I want to glass from the standing position, I rest the binocular on that padded hiking stick. Otherwise, I steady the binocular by resting both elbows on my thighs above the knees. A shaky picture makes wildlife discovery painfully difficult, and can lead to a headache as the image dances before your eyes.

With steady body and steady binocular, take in the whole view. Scan over the landscape. Experience will tell you where to look for what. Sometimes that's obvious. If you're looking for hawk nests along a river, check the cliffs. If you want to locate rabbits in a noonday desert draw, look into the shady spots. A binocular naturally isolates the viewing area. So the next step is to look intently within the field of the glass, not swinging the glass itself back and forth, but allowing your eyes to do the moving within the framework of the field of view.

When searching for wildlife, focus and refocus the image from soft focus (a slightly fuzzy image) to hard focus (a sharp image). Many times, this tactic will reveal the texture of a questionable object in the distance. The little rock by the big rock may turn out to be a bedded fox, for example, if you soft-focus and hard-focus on it.

Look for the part, not the whole, just as you would without the glass. Many animals have identifying minifeatures. A pronghorn antelope, for example, may appear as a white dot, especially if the erectile rump guard hairs are standing out. A cream-colored patch could be a mule deer. Look for the smallest of things. I was recently glassing an area not far from my home when I noticed a shiny object in a grassy field. It could have been a piece of glass, but it wasn't. It was a whitetailed deer bedded right in the middle of a cultivated field.

The same day, another glint in the brush proved to be a badger. Their shiny eyes gave these animals away. Look for motion, too, as you would without the glass — that tail twitch, ear flick, eye flash. And search for shapes, the shape of an ear in the brush, the arch of a back, horizontal lines among so many vertical lines.

Wildlife watching means just that — watching. And it is often the binocular that brings that wildlife opportunity and visual experience right into your lap.

RECORDABLE OBSERVATIONS

Look back at the wildlife notebook and you will see how that written record coincides perfectly with becoming a better observer of wildlife. Naturally, all of the interesting behaviors, as well as the addition of another sighting are recordable in your book of wildlife experiences.

CONCLUSION

Man seems to have traded instinct for intellect. While we are the smartest animal, we are not the best equipped for the outdoor environment in which we now find ourselves only visitors. And that includes our ability to perceive the great outdoors. But through conscious effort, we can vastly improve our visual acuity and awareness. We may act as "understudy" to a partner who has more knowledge than we have in wildlife watching; he can help us to heighten our wildlife-spotting ability. And through continued practice, enhanced experience, and the wise use of a few tools, especially the binocular, we can gain proficiency in becoming more aware of the wild creatures around us.

3

Project Sound Waves

INTRODUCTION

We were standing in a meadow at the edge of town. My friend, an avid wildlife watcher, stood still as a granite boulder as he perched his binoculars atop a special factory-made walking staff. He even had eye black, à la football players, smeared under each eye to absorb any extraneous light that might be reflected from his cheekbones and impair his vision.

After he had looked long enough at the object of his interest, he turned to me. "Let's sit down over there so I can record this while it's fresh in my mind. Did you see those guys go at it? I couldn't tell if they hurt each other, but the way they lunged and rolled, I wouldn't be surprised." He was describing the actions of a couple of semidomestic squirrels that were behaving like school kids thirty seconds after the dismissal bell. My friend wrote his observations in detail, then handed them to me.

"Good notes," I said. And they were. "But I think you left something out."

"Left out what?" my friend challenged.

"The most memorable part," I said. "The noise."

My friend's notes did not contain a single word to describe sounds. His observations had been on a silent screen. Several years ago, mine would have been, too. The voice of a child had changed my silent notes into "talkies." My little girl's notebook—she was about seven years old at the time—had a series of squiggly marks on one page. I asked her what those marks were. "They show what the birds were saying," she answered.

"Hmmm. Yes. I see," I replied. "So they do."

Fine-tuning ourselves to the outdoors means far more than increasing our ability to see wild creatures, although *seeing* certainly comprises the main objective of most outings. Just as we learn to see more acutely outdoors, we also learn to hear more acutely. It is just as precise a project as any other, and its rewards are just as great.

The human being is capable of rather decent hearing ability. Evolutionists believe that the human ear has evolved negatively, that once it had a large pinna, or outer ear, and that the fold of skin called the helix, now no more than a vistigial line on the upper part of the pinna, was once much larger than its present size. Perhaps the outer ear was directional, too. The human could rotate his ear about in all directions in order to better funnel in various sound waves, not only to interpret them, but also to locate the direction from which they came.

I don't know about the evolutionary aspect of human hearing, but when compared with the lower animals, our ears aren't all that sensitive. And yet, we can still hear very well. We hear best in a range of about 1,000 to 5,000 cycles (the rate of vibration of any sound: the higher the number of cycles, the higher the pitch). Scientists are not exactly sure, but it seems that other mammals may hear up to 60,000 cycles, perhaps higher. Our inability to hear a dog whistle is a good example of how, compared to other animals, our hearing is limited.

There are three major ways to improve our hearing ability outdoors—one is with hardware, another is through specific methods of listening and the third is through field practice.

OBJECT OF THE PROJECT

What are we listening for? The obvious answer is wildlife. We listen for the songs of birds in the city park and in our backyards. We listen for the cry of the hunting hawk, the howl of the coyote, the mating

We listen for many things, including the songs of birds, that can both teach and delight us.

"whistle" of the bull elk. These wonderful sounds are only a microcosm of the seemingly limitless sounds of the wildworld, however.

By employing the methods described below, you may discover a world of sound previously unknown to you—water dashing its way down a creek path, the trees rubbing against themselves in the wind, the sun warming the land.

You *can* hear the sun warming the land. The heat makes objects expand, and as they do, there is sound. And there is sound as objects cool. I have heard a crack in the forest so loud that it seemed a tree was falling, yet it was only the reaction of that tree to its loss of internal heat—the contraction of the bark or other parts of the tree made the loud snap!

But you say you have always listened to all of these things. True. Now learn to *hear* them. There is a vast difference between listening and hearing. Becoming more sensitive to the sounds of nature is a fantastic experience for the human ear.

The object of this project is to increase your ability to hear the important sounds that flow to you constantly outdoors. Your ears collect all of the sounds within the human range and the range of your personal hearing ability. A vital aspect of this project is the interpretation of those sounds.

By following the precepts laid out here, you can increase your ability to hear messages outdoors. We learn how to hear better outdoors by fine-tuning our ability to hear. It is imperative to focus your listening, just as you focus a binocular. Listen to the sounds of a busy street, and you hear . . . noise. Listen with a "focused ear," and you hear people talking, feet shuffling, papers rattling, wheels turning, engines humming, wind blowing, horns sounding.

The enchantment of wildwood sounds is richer yet. I have heard a black bear clawing its way up a tree, whitetailed bucks clashing antlers in the thicket, bighorn sheep rams crashing horns, water drops falling from leaves, and much more. Few animals are mute. Most have a replete vocabulary of sound.

The crack of a stick as a big animal moves through the woods, a wild turkey luring a mate, birds at the feeder speaking with excitement over a new find of seeds, a beaver cutting the water on an early evening pond or smacking its tail against the surface, a squirrel declaring its boundaries—these are but a few of the notes from an outdoor concert written on sheet music anyone can afford.

Wind makes the habitat speak, too, as does water in motion. But you have to focus. You have to channel the sound waves. And that is the object of this proj-

ect—to become more sensitive to, and to better interpret, data gathered by your ear.

Knowing the sounds of the outdoors helps us not only in locating wild creatures, but also in identifying them. We must be aware of the individual sounds that come to us disguised as a blend. Sounds can tell us of the presence of wildlife and also of its location and distance from us, but we can be fooled. I once heard the language of feeding Canada geese. The sounds came through as if isolated in headphones. I thought they must be only a few hundred feet away. I walked a half mile or more but could not locate the flock. Another half mile. Nothing. And then, there the birds were, feeding in a field. Their language had revealed their presence, but they were a full mile farther away than I thought when I first heard their communications carried to my ears on the clear air.

Nonetheless, we very often pinpoint the distance as well as the direction of a wildwatch candidate by first hearing its voice. Perceptive ears are an asset in all wildlife watching. There is a reverse benefit here, too. Once we learn to hear better outdoors, our appreciation for the advanced hearing ability of wild animals is upgraded. Such appreciation makes us better wildlife watchers.

EQUIPMENT

Few pieces of hardware are required to enhance the wildlife watcher's ability to hear better in the outdoors, and that hardware is inexpensive. First, consider an animal's ear. It is more complex than a bird's ear, which, by virtue of its design, does not require a large pinna (outer ear) to collect sound. The animal's ear often has a large outer "sound collector," and it is

The mammalian ear is directional and can move about to concentrate incoming sound waves. This ear also has a large pinna to better collect sound.

directional in nature. We know this from watching our pets. A dog cocks his head toward the sound in order to gather up every nuance of information coming on the air waves.

The human ear is also complex, but its pinna is small compared with that of a bat, deer, rabbit, or other animal. We can benefit, then, from a sound-gathering device to compensate for our small pinna.

The main tool we will use is our hands. Three other tools can also be used: the "elephant ear," the horn, and the hearing aid. The elephant ear is simply a large cardboard pinna with a hole in it. This can be made in many ways. One simple way is to dampen cardboard and press it into a bowl. Apply glue to the damp cardboard (on the exposed side only) as it rests in the bowl. After drying, the cardboard will retain the shape of the bowl. Cut a half-inch-diameter hole in the center of the cardboard, which is now shaped somewhat like a pinna. We'll talk more of the elephant ear when I discuss methods of gaining more acute auditory perception.

The hearing horn is just that—a horn. It, too, can be made of damp cardboard. Lighter gauge cardboard works best. Simply roll the cardboard into the shape of a cornucopia and let it dry. In days of yore, a cow horn, sometimes with a rubber tip to be inserted into the ear, was often used as a hearing aid. These horns worked well. It is quite possible to locate cow horn today, and you need only cut the smaller end for a comfortable fit against the ear. Either one of these horns will suffice.

I do not recommend a hearing aid for

An "elephant ear" can be made by pressing wet cardboard into a bowl or, as shown here, by preparing one from papier-mâché.

An old plastic bowl with a hole cut in its center makes an excellent elephant ear for capturing the sounds of the wild.

I have a wildlife trail I travel in winter. Sometimes the trail is covered with a fresh blanket of snow; usually it is not. When it isn't, my boots often "talk" too much as they make contact with the ground. I acquired a pair of Coleman Snow Joggers, a sneaker-type shoe with a quiet sole and a bit of insulation against the cold. They are perfect on my winter wildlife trail. The connection is real; a quiet person hears more. Clothing that is quiet actually is a listening tool.

A final tool that will aid in wildlife listening is the tape recorder. Its use is described below.

METHODS AND PROCEDURES

This project may be enjoyed in any outdoor setting, from the backyard to the nearby city park to the most remote wilderness area. The first step in learning to

sound enhancement because of its expense, but it deserves mention. A hearing aid can heighten your ability to hear in the wild by enhancing wildlife sounds. If you happen to wear a hearing aid already, remember to take it with you on your wildlife forays.

Indirectly, the other tools of hearing enhancement are those items of clothing that make us quieter in the outdoors and more comfortable. As with binocular use, the observer who is not comfortable simply cannot concentrate properly, and it takes concentration to absorb the messages of the wildwood. Why quiet? That's simple. If you are making noise as you move through the environment, that noise masks all other sounds.

ActionEar is an electronic device that amplifies incoming sounds for the wildwatcher and therefore aids in location and identification of wildlife.

listen better outdoors is to remain still. Stand or sit quietly; do not move; do not talk. Failure to be quiet cancels out all careful listening techniques. A person in motion hears far less than a person at rest. So when you want to hear the most, stop walking, stop everything, remain quiet. That's all. To hear the difference, take a short stroll in your backyard or along your sidewalk. Listen as you walk. Now stop and listen again. You'll hear more once you stop moving.

The second step is to concentrate on the sounds permeating the environment. This is vital because, just as the blended sounds on a city street become noise, so do the many blended sounds of the outdoors meld into a cacophony of sound. Perhaps cacophony is the wrong term. It is only discord to the wildlife observer who has not learned to sort out the sounds. To hear birds singing is nice, but you can't learn much from the songs, unless you can interpret them. Remember that our objective is to pinpoint and identify subjects of observation through our ability to hear. That takes concentration and practice.

After learning to concentrate your sense of hearing, the third step is to sort out each individual sound. Make a list — mental or written — of the number of different sounds you can sift from the entire range of sound coming to you on a given day in a given area. Recording such auditory data is discussed below, but for now, a simple list will do. The number of wildlife and outdoor sounds that can be heard in a tiny woodlot in your neighborhood is amazing. To test my own advice, I proceeded to a pond no more than 600 paces from my home; around that pond I catalogued 67 different sounds in a very short period of time.

Fourth, try the elephant ear and listen-

The Coleman Snow Jogger is one type of new footwear that can make the wildwatcher more comfortable and quieter in the outdoors.

ing horns described above. These directional devices are merely held to the ear so that sound is funneled through them, taking the place of the large outer ear enjoyed by so many other mammals. You may also want to use the hearing aid alone or in conjunction with the elephant ear, paper horn, or cow horn hearing devices.

The fifth step, and by far most important part of the project, is the use of cupped hands. These tools are with us all the time and are used by simply holding a hand around each ear. Cupped hands do more than exaggerate our abbreviated pinnas; they also aid greatly in concentrating our attention on individual pieces of the habitat before us. With a hand cupped about each ear, slowly turn your whole body through a complete circle. This action further segments the field into individual areas to be studied and makes the additional outer ear surfaces very directional in nature — a major goal in listening.

Initially, the simple matter of cupping hands to aid hearing can produce almost

By simply cupping hands around your ears, you magnify the effectiveness of your outer ear. Your ability to determine the direction of sound will also increase.

startling results. I was standing in a mountain meadow one time, having looked for a stream for two hours. The topographical map showed the stream to be nearby, but I wasn't exactly sure how many more canyons I would have to cross before finding the waterway. I cupped my hands around my ears, and the rush of water came to me instantly. I pivoted my head around slowly and soon had the exact location of the stream pinpointed.

I have no idea how many times I have cupped hands to magnify wild animal sounds. It works not only to reveal animal noises but to enhance all outdoor sounds. This method of heightening hearing ability remains my favorite.

RECORDABLE OBSERVATIONS

Animals have a language of their own. In the strictest sense, the linguistic scientist may not agree, but anyone who has watched domestic or wild creatures will certainly attest to a communication among them. It takes no special knowledge to distinguish the differences among various dog barks, for example. "Play with me" sounds very different from "There's an intruder outside the door."

I once had the privilege of listening to a wild black bear making a sound I can describe only as a purr. I was further privileged to experience a different sound coming from that same bear when another blackie disturbed him.

The different sounds we hear outdoors should be recorded. The tape recorder is the best way to record the sounds of the wildworld. Later in this book an entire project will be devoted to the use of the tape recorder in capturing the auditory messages passing from one wild creature to another. For now, suffice it to say that recorded audio tapes of various animal communications can make a very interesting library.

Most of us will want to record in our notebooks the highlights of what we hear in the field. This means that a special vocabulary will have to be established. Such a vocabulary is generally a personal shorthand of sound. One early evening, I was enjoying a backpack camp-out in a rather remote area of the west. The packing was easy, and I had with me most of the amenities of the trail, even my favorite folding stove. The stove, placed in front of my lean-to, generated plenty of warmth, and I lay back in total comfort. I decided to catalogue the sounds coming from the lake shore.

At that point, I realized that my own shorthand of animal sounds had a fairly universal "ring" to it. We have established many, many onomatopoeic words, words that symbolize a given sound. Crack! You can hear the twig break. Grrrr! You can hear the bear growl. Screee! The hunting hawk announces her presence. Chip! Chip! A squirrel chatters from a treetop. These are descriptive sounds, and when we run out of them, it's easy to come up with other terms to describe noises. "The stream sounded like a dozen fire hoses cutting away at the side of the hill." There is no mistaking this rushing water for a gentle, gurgling trickle.

The goal in recording sounds is to actually learn what the animals are "saying." To insist that the lower animals have no real communication is far more foolhardy than making too much of their language. Porpoises and whales are not alone in having extensive vocabularies. Over only one hill from my home is a small colony of

Take a stand in any area where there is wildlife and record the sounds you hear.

The scree! of the eagle is just one of the wildlife sounds awaiting the naturalist who uses his ears as well as his eyes in the outdoors.

prairie dogs. In watching and listening to them, I never have to see the hawk that floats overhead. The alarm cry of the prairie dog conveys the message as surely as if it were a human voice speaking English.

The sounds of wildlife can be an entire study of its own. But the sounds must be recorded, preferably on audio cassettes. Bird sounds, especially, are far too complicated to record with pen and ink. Students of animal sounds have learned that bird songs vary in meaning. One song may be an auditory method of marking off a territory; another may be an entirely different message for other birds.

You can listen to the tape over and over again, until patterns are identified. The sound can also be slowed in speed or raised in volume until you grasp the vocabulary of the birds. There are ornithologists and birdwatchers who do an excellent job of noting bird calls in writing. But for the everyday wildlife watcher, the tape recorder renders a totally faithful reproduction of those calls.

CONCLUSION

The values of acute auditory perception are evident. A few simple tools can aid the cause, but even these can be dispensed with, except for the quiet shoes and clothing. Quietness, cupped hands, concentration, and a step-by-step approach to a greater awareness of wildwood sounds are all the tools required by the wildlife watcher who wants to sensitize his hearing abilities. It all seems so simple because it *is* simple. But without self-training, the average visitor to the outdoors will hear only a cacophony of noises—a conglomerate of many individual sounds—rather than the entire wildwood language passing among the animals.

4

Project On the Wind

INTRODUCTION

Man ranks toward the bottom of the list in his ability to gather information through his olfactory abilities, that is, his sense of smell. Because we are not expected to use our noses to gather information in the outdoors, we often don't even try. We assume that it would be hopeless to attempt to discover very much in this manner, so we go about ignoring one of the five major senses with which we are blessed.

This is a minor tragedy for the sincere wildlife watcher, because using the sense of smell enhances the outdoor adventure not only through a greater enjoyment of that world, but also through a far better understanding of nature. Why? Because the wild creatures we enjoy watching and photographing rely heavily upon the sense of smell in their everyday lives. This is not

so true of the birds as it is of animals, of course, but to fail to recognize that the world of wildlife is replete with information to be gained through the nose is to lack understanding of a powerful force acting upon all wildlife.

Conversely, once we apply our own abilities to gather messages coming to us on the outdoor breezes, then we begin to better understand the great force these messages have on the wild folk that live outside our door. For many years I have attempted to refine my own sense of smell. The rewards have been great, and I wish to share them with you.

Aromas constitute a full dimension of the outdoor experience. Ignoring them is like pinching our nostrils shut while we eat our dinner. Not *all* of our sense of taste would disappear if we obstructed our sense of smell, but much of it would. We

Wild animals, especially mammals, rely heavily on the sense of smell for detection of danger "on the wind" and for mating success.

have all heard of, or perhaps have been a part of, the experiment in which a tiny segment of apple is placed on the tongue of a person whose sense of smell has been blocked, followed by a tiny bit of onion. A person denied his ability to smell may not know which is the onion, which is the apple.

I say *"may* not," because the ability to detect various aromas varies with individuals. There are persons who have a rather acute sense of smell and others who have a hard time distinguishing one odor from another. Most of us have sufficient ability to detect considerable information on the winds of the wild places, as well as in our local parks and nearby woodlots, and it's a shame to waste that talent. Remember that to better understand your own sensitivity to the odors of the world is to better understand the tremendous impact that

a multitude of aromas imposes upon the wildworld. To fail in this understanding is to leave an entire dimension out of the wildlife-watching picture.

OBJECT OF THE PROJECT

The major goal of this project is to make you more aware of your sense of smell and to encourage you to use this sense to the fullest in your wildwatching. If you improve your ability to appreciate and decipher the messages of odors, you will have opened another small but very important door to outdoor enjoyment and wildlife understanding.

I was in the Southern Arizona desert a good many years ago, collecting reptiles for a classroom project. The students were learning various behavior patterns of snakes, particularly the rattlesnake. The snakes were kept in glass aquariums for a two-month period before being released back into their natural environment. It was now time to return a couple of especially large specimens to the wild. I had both in one gunnysack. They were cool from the early morning temperature and from being in the shade of the car; I expected no problem in releasing them. However, I had forgotten one small detail—the area I originally found them in and to which they were now being returned was filled with many similar reptiles.

It was, in effect, one big rockpile. I climbed up into the rocks, the gunnysack gently hoisted to avoid bruising the live contents of the bag. My concentration was on the sack, not on the ground in front of me. I did not see the big rattler; I smelled him. An indescribable odor came to my nostrils and hit me directly in the face. The rattlesnake "perfume" reminded me of a buck goat's pungent essence, an aroma I had learned to identify from my brother's prize goats. I paused, looking all around, and then I saw him. Right in front of me on the next rock was a thick-bodied diamondback rattler, warming in the early sun. I might have put a hand right on the fellow had my nose not warned me off.

A further objective of this project is to heighten our awareness of animal response to scent. This is done by furthering our own sensitivity to aromas of the wild. My rattlesnake encounter was a rare case of man using his ability to detect odors in order to safeguard his welfare. Birds, and especially mammals, do this very thing all the time. In many instances, the sense of smell is a number-one early warning device.

If you intend to get close to the animals you wish to watch or photograph, a full understanding of their ability to read the airwaves for different messages is imperative. The upcoming signpost project is based entirely upon the fact that wild animals depend on their sense of smell to inform them of their world.

Finally, it is the objective of this project to increase your general enjoyment of the wilds through a greater awareness of the many essences present there. We have become desensitized to many aromas because our sense of smell is bombarded daily with many unpleasant odors such as tobacco, smog, dust, among others. If we give our sense of smell a chance, it will improve somewhat as we enjoy wildlife watching outdoors because the nasal passages tend to clear to a degree when cleansed by unpolluted air.

Don't give up if at first your nose does not respond to the information presented to it in the wild. The sense of smell re-

The many "unnatural" odors of civilization have desensitized our sense of smell. It takes practice to be able to gain information from nature through our noses.

One reason for developing our sense of smell is to increase our enjoyment of the outdoors. A bit of sagebrush crushed between the fingers gives off a pungent aroma.

treats from offending odors. Peel onions, and for the first few moments the odor is penetrating. Given time, you notice the pungent odor less and less. You simply get used to the smell. Our noses are used to the many artificial odors of civilization and it takes a little time away from these essences before we can appreciate the newsworthy bits of information stimulating our nasal passages.

EQUIPMENT

No special equipment is needed for this project, except for the ever-present wildlife watcher's notebook, which accompanies all of our efforts.

METHODS AND PROCEDURES

The title of this project, On the Wind, has special significance, because just as we hike *downwind* to avoid having wild animals detect our presence before we can study them, we hike *upwind* to learn more through our noses as we study an ecological niche.

The first step in gaining an appreciation for the messages of different odors is to take a little outing—you need not go far. You will be able to enjoy an environment replete with natural aromas wherever city smells do not totally dominate. Any ecological niche will do. The seashore is blessed with many different aromas, from salt water to various sea life, both plant and animal. When the tide goes out, the beach becomes an entire diary of different odors. The high mountains offer another set of odors to study, from the damp earth around a stream, pond, or lake to the trees that grow there.

Having arrived in the project area, give your sense of smell a chance to adjust to the peculiar aromas and to forget the many odors of the city. The most important part of this project is to allow your sense of smell to function. Modern man has all but forgotten how to sort tidbits of information from odors present in the environment.

Play a little game. Close your eyes and try to list all of the different messages that your nose can decipher. After this little exercise, get up and wander about. You will meet with more different outdoor aromas than this book can possibly list. The most telling of these aromas generally emanate from the larger mammals.

Elk and moose have distinctive essences that the wind picks up. Many times I have smelled the presence or recent presence of both of these big quadrupeds. Deer may also leave messages about themselves on the wind or rubbed on the rocks, trees, and bushes of the area. Rutting animals tend to emit more powerful calling cards. The scent glands of the deer, for example, may send forth sufficient essence to be recognized by the human nose.

Of course, there are some especially odorous little fellows that anybody can detect. The peccary of the Southwest and Mexico is one such creature. A musk-hog, these small piglike animals have a large scent gland located on their upper posteriors. Some naturalists believe that the glandular odors from this musk sac are used to help keep the animals grouped together, since they roam in packs, and since they have very weak eyesight. The skunk, of course, can leave enough of itself behind to be easily recognized. There are many smaller animals that also have strong scent glands, but the messages they leave are too discreet for us to detect.

Earth, special tree bark, certain leaves, pine needles, mushrooms, sap, lichen, moss, wild mint (particularly aromatic), rain, prerain, and after-rain perfumes—

Most mammals have real "radar noses" with long nasal passages. Even the great Jimmy Durante's nose was nothing in comparison to this badger's.

these are all picked up by any human nose, even when that nose has grown used to the many powerful smells of the city. So the "sniff-out" procedure is usually very basic and simple—a matter of refining our awareness of the many messages we can receive through our sense of smell.

RECORDABLE OBSERVATIONS

Making long lists of detected aromas is not necessary. For the younger wildlife watcher, such lists may at first serve to enhance awareness of the many messages to be found in odors, of course, and as such can be encouraged. But the seasoned nature lover need not embark upon a strict cataloguing routine. By the same token, notes replete with visual observations, and even records of sounds, but without so much as a mention of wildwood aromas, are not complete notes. Because animals react to smells, their behavior can often be predicted or explained if we know what odors are present.

Consider the dog as it senses fear in a

human being. Perhaps an animal can sense fear in a person because it detects a change in the individual's odor. Even though fear causes a flow of adrenaline, I do not believe that added adrenaline in the system can actually be detected by the nostrils of another animal. Some naturalists think so, however. We do know that sweat glands may react to alterations in mood, and this emission is no doubt a telling sign to any animal. It is an aroma even the human nose readily identifies.

The frightened wild animal often emits an odor, though it is not the odor of sweat. The classic example is the skunk.

Man has no problem recognizing that a skunk has been aroused. And have you ever smelled the little weasel? Get close enough to a weasel when it's alarmed, and your nose will detect a change in the condition of the air. Most mammals emit similar bodily aromas. We humans simply don't detect them. But other animals, with real radar noses, do. Remember that. What a skunk does to your nose, a mouse can do in a less dramatic way to the sensitive nostrils of a coyote or wolf.

Leaving such details out of wildlife notes is missing the mark by a wide margin. I was trying to photograph, without

A scrape like this one with droppings in it leaves a strong olfactory message for other members of the herd that pass by the territory of the buck that left this marker.

Scent plays an important role in the deer's mating cycle. Glands emit various essences that attract the opposite sex, and the bucks mark off a territory with scent.

any real success, the rutting of the little Southwestern Coues deer several years ago. The deer were highly visible, a rather unusual circumstance for this wary animal. However, getting close enough for a truly good frame-filling photograph was impossible. But the wildlife watching was very interesting, and most of it was launched by scent trails and noses. The scent trails left by the does were easily followed by the bucks. A buck would briskly walk the side of a hill, head held high, and then his nose would dive downward as if an invisible string had lowered his head with a jerk.

Off he'd go, trailing the scent as surely as a hound. It was interesting to watch the deer going through the antics of romance, but it took only moments to note an even more interesting factor, the path and pattern executed by the doe in estrus. The circuitous routes wound around and around, but generally along an established trail. Occasionally the path would lead across an open hillside, then emerge once more on a path. I was recording animal movement, but the impetus behind the trailing was definitely an odor. Many activities of wild creatures are just that — reactions to a world of odors. It takes a bit

Many wildlife creatures rely heavily on their noses for information.

of careful observation, but soon you will realize that the action and reaction of your subjects are often ruled more by the nose than by the eyes.

To ignore such recordable observations is to leave, not the icing off the cake, but the cake out from beneath the icing. So I always catalogue aromas, especially when the aromas are clearly the very *cause* of what I am watching. Of course, a cause/effect relationship is not always clear. I noted an extremely interesting series of

events relating to a rather elaborate system of bird feeders a friend had set up. The feeder consisted of four different stations — two loaded with general birdseed that finches and sparrows were attracted to and two with sunflower seeds, of more interest to the grosbeaks that were in the area. My friend called to tell me that something interesting was happening. The two lower feeders were no longer being used by the birds.

I had no clue that would unravel the

mystery. My friend watched the feeders religiously but learned nothing until one morning before work when he noticed a fluffy neighbor cat crawling all over one of the lower feeders. The clever cat found he could gain the feeder by making a running leap and attaching himself with unsheathed claws to the bottom of the unit, then chinning himself onto the platform of the feeder itself. How come the birds quit using the feeder, even when the cat was nowhere to be seen? A bird's sense of smell is not supposed to be that keen, but my best guess rests with this answer—the birds could detect catscent on the two lower feeders. It was that scent keeping them away.

A similar incident took place at a water hole built by another wildlife-watching enthusiast. He knew that the area was loaded with wildlife, but his water hole was not a success until he realized that his pet collie had marked the territory off completely. He restrained the dog, and within a week the water hole was busy. There is much cause and effect related to odors in the world of wildlife. Recogniz-ing, understanding, and recording these actions is an important part of any wild-life notebook.

CONCLUSION

Of the five major senses known to the animal world, man probably relies less on his nose and related taste buds than upon the other three major receivers of stimuli; even his hearing and his touch get more attention. The wildworld, however, is re-plete with olfactory messages; wild ani-mals rely heavily upon these messages and react to them constantly. To ignore these powerful stimuli is to deny a very impor-tant aspect of wildlife watching. Through a specific process of increasing awareness, you can vastly improve your ability to dis-cover the perfumes of nature through your sense of smell. You will also learn vastly more about wildlife subjects by recogniz-ing how many aspects of their lives are guided by what no one can see—those little clues without size, shape, or color—the essences that guide, rule, and com-mand so much in nature.

5

Project Daytrip for Habitat

INTRODUCTION

You have been honing your wildlife-watching senses and building your skills, often in a backyard setting, the nearby park, or any other ecological niche near your home. This start-up project doesn't draw you far away either; it's designed as a one-day outing into nearby habitat. It serves, however, to give you, the wildlife observer, a place of your own in which you know the ropes, the lay of the land, and the wildlife that dwells there. The project has several important benefits. But before going into the details, a suggestion—observe but do not disturb. Observe the wild creatures in their natural setting, but do not chase them, especially in wintertime when the loss of energy could result in serious consequences.

I was enjoying a walk along a snow trail in a large park one winter. It was easy going; the snow was fresh but light, and a pair of hiking boots sufficed for comfort. This lowland country, through which a river flowed, was home to many white-tailed deer, and the clan had gathered together, or "yarded," as is their usual habit in winter. There were, without exaggeration, a few hundred deer within an area of no more than a few hundred acres.

The quiet was broken by the din of two snowmobiles. Snowmobiles are excellent winter transportation, superior recreation vehicles, and generally no real threat to the environment. The two persons riding these snowmobiles, however, were in an area where wildlife was grouped into a critical winter range. Furthermore, although the snow was light and the weather relatively mild, the males of the herd had not too long ago been in the rut. Their body fat was sub-par. Food was not abun-

In winter wild animals can be under particularly high stress. They should not be chased or frightened into running. This wastes their precious energy. With care, and a telephoto lens, wildlife, such as this antelope herd, can be observed and photographed without being disturbed.

dant, as is typical of winterland settings, and the animals were surviving by saving their energy.

The snowmobiles put the herd I was watching into full flight. The animals darted back and forth among the trees of the river bottom, panicked by the sudden approach of two fast-moving objects gliding over the snow. While the snowmobilers would normally have been no problem, their intrusion on the resting deer caused an energy-wasting situation for the animals. Someone on foot in that locale could easily "spook" the animals, too, but not into headlong flight. In fact, when I located another herd later in the day, the animals saw me but didn't bolt. They turned and *walked* into the trees.

Observe, but do not disturb.

OBJECT OF THE PROJECT

A very important objective drives this project — the location of wildlife-watching habitat. But even more than that, it encourages a systematic and orderly perusal of an area so that wildwatching will be not only enjoyable but also recordable. This can be one of the most interesting projects of all, because it is an adventure in *discovery*. The project also promotes a healthy walk in the outdoors.

On the trail, use a fanny pack for carrying gear that is essential for safety and comfort.

EQUIPMENT

The daytrip for wildlife habitat discovery requires the normal equipment used for any outing—clothes and boots, quiet and befitting the weather conditions, and the usual outdoor gear necessary for any daytrip. Take along either a daypack or fanny pack to carry your lunch, a flashlight—just in case you get so interested in wildlife watching that you're late in returning to your car—a small first-aid kit, and hardware suited to any type of hike. Don't forget your binoculars and camera!

METHODS AND PROCEDURES

The first step in seeking your special wildlife-watching habitat begins by recog-

nizing the goal, which is to locate negotiable and accessible wildlife-rich environments not too far from home. Land status is paramount to the success of this project. Do not trespass on private land; ask permission of the landowner before embarking on any wildlife watch. One of my favorite areas begins where my backyard leaves off, a private ranch adjoined to our out-of-city subdivision. I explained to the landowner that I wanted to study and photograph wildlife, nothing more. He said OK after I told him that I would faithfully follow his rules, which were: do not drive off the roads and into the pastures (I was on foot anyway); leave closed gates shut, opened gates open; and do not engage in rockhounding, because the area

A daypack holds even more of the essentials of outdoor life.

contained various Indian artifacts he did not want disturbed.

Wildlife habitat is public or private in status. Public lands include U.S. Forest Service areas; national, state, and local parks; Bureau of Land Management (BLM) acreage; declared wilderness regions; wildlife sanctuaries; and other properties granted public access. The Audubon Society, as well as local bird-watching groups, may help you locate public areas for wildwatching. Also, contact farmers and ranchers for permission to wildwatch on private property. Buy a map of your intended wildlife area. You will need the map, not only for orienta-

Many well-maintained wildlife areas exist close to town. Be sure to take advantage of any information provided with these trailsites and special areas.

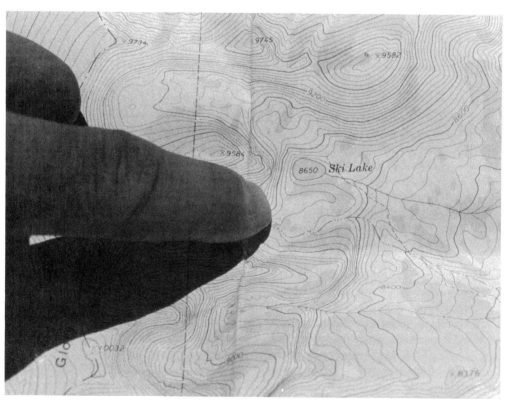

Topographical maps are a boon to any wildwatcher. These maps are especially useful for locating watersites and roads and for becoming familiar with the general "lay of the land."

tion, but also as a part of the upcoming recordable data section of this project.

Study your map before leaving home. A topographical map will show you the various changes in elevation and, in essence, the differences in vegetation in each locality. The map will reveal various types of habitat and illustrate waterways, roads, trails, and buildings. Use the map wisely. It can lead you to the best possible wildlife-watching niches in the general region. Your goal, remember, is the orderly discovery of wildlife habitat, and the word *orderly* is used to denote a careful and systematic approach.

I begin by looking for water sites — streams, lakes, rivers, even the tiniest ponds. The watery places often hold special nesting and bird staging areas. Plus they hold sign in the soft, damp earth around them. (Sign is the evidence left behind by animals or birds, including tracks; feathers; hair rubbed off on rocks, branches, or fences; excreta; scrapes; and rubs.) Water sites often have special foliage that offers cover for wildlife. I look for any trails. Some regions have well-established trails created especially for public enjoyment of the area.

A mountainous chunk of land just outside of Salt Lake City, Utah, offers a network of maintained trails for hikers and wildlife watchers, which I enjoyed one summer. These trails were literally minutes away from town. Your region may also have established trail networks near home.

Now go about the *orderly and systematic* search for the best wildwatch environments in the area. Look with care; you may enjoy these areas for decades to come. As you hike into the land, use each and every asset described in previous projects. Don't just see the area, experience it visually — use those binoculars. Listen to the region as it "talks" to you.

Don't ignore the natural aromas present everywhere. Feel the outdoors, the texture of a leaf or the breeze on your face. This sort of approach will offer a relaxed and enjoyable outing — the true *recreation* mentioned in the Foreword.

Of course, you don't always have to walk in order to have excellent outdoor exercise. The advent of the mountain bicycle allows you to ride the trails. I can see no harm done to the wildwood with such a bicycle, with the possible exception of putting ruts into a muddy trail.

It's necessary to discuss another aspect of learning the regions that offer the best wildlife watching. Even though these regions are usually quite close to home, a number of wildlife lovers have gotten lost in pursuit of their hobby. It's not that difficult to do. You become engrossed in the activity; you see a nesting bird, a feeding deer, general wild animal movement and interaction, even the industry of insects. The next thing you know, you've lost your way. Since our daytrip for wildlife does not require long-distance hiking, I suggest "keeping found" by the very simplest of methods.

Forget your natural instinct or sense of direction. I believe that some people truly do have a perspective of the land that prevents them from getting lost easily, but when the U.S. Army ran its survival school in the Yuma, Arizona, desert, it was soon discovered that humans have very little sense of direction. Blindfolded, most of the participants could not maintain a straight line while walking. They circled — some to the left, some to the right — but none walked straight ahead.

Forget, too, the idea of which side of the tree the moss grows on or how the prevailing winds blow in that region. I do not discount either; however, for our purposes I offer simpler methods.

Use a path. An authorized trail open to the public is great for wildlife watching. Anyone can remain "found" if he stays on a trail. If the trail is convoluted, offering numerous forks along the way, it is perfectly acceptable to mark the correct return. Just be sure to retrieve the markers on the way back. Blaze-orange streamers are litter when left behind. Or follow the shore of a lake; stay to a stream bed; remain in a canyon. Take note of large, obvious landmarks and keep them in sight.

Walk parallel with a road, keeping the road in sight most of the time. There is a multitude of interesting wildlife along most roadways in our countryside. A friend of mine who resides in New Jersey along a major highway has catalogued over a hundred wildlife species within view of that ribbon of asphalt.

It's OK to use the sun as a directional aid, but don't get fancy. If you walk into the sun, time yourself. After you have hiked with the sun in your face for an hour, you know that you must hike for an hour with the sun at your back, maintaining about the same pace, until you reach your starting point.

RECORDABLE OBSERVATIONS

Your daytrip for habitat will reward you with many observations to record in the notebook you prepared for Project Wild-

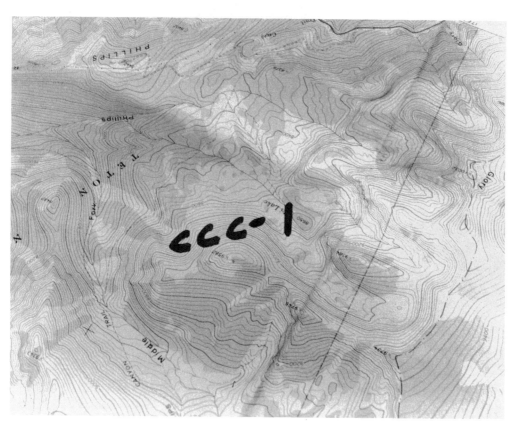

A wildwatcher may wish to mark his topo maps with his own code in order to classify various areas.

watch Diary. However, this project also includes building your personal wildlife-observation maps. The codes you use on your maps should correspond with your notebook as part of your record of wildlife observation. There are basically two types of wildlife observation maps, the personal map you make yourself (be it no more than pencil lines outlining the special habitats you enjoy) and commercial topographical maps upon which you jot your own notes.

Here is an example of a map-record. I have a topographical map that includes a stream, and upon it I have marked CCC-1, p. 77; CCC-7, p. 94; CCC-9, p. 119.

The page number refers to my wildwatch diary. I can turn to page 77 and find out what was happening with subject CCC on a specific date. That gives me a time frame and an explanation of events. The CCC-1 in this instance refers to my first sighting of the subject in that locale; CCC-7 is my seventh sighting of the same subject, in this case in the exact same location on the map. CCC happens to be a red fox den located on an open flat next to a stream. By all means, you should devise your own system, but I suggest you start it on the daytrip for habitat. There is no better time.

A simple coding of the map may con-

You don't necessarily have to go far to enjoy wildwatching. Many interesting creatures, such as these antelope, may sometimes be observed at a local park.

tain numbers and nothing more. For example, a topographical map of a given area may be marked 1 through 41. These numbers refer to events that are recorded in the notebook. Number 1 may be a sighting with explanatory notes concerning a nesting eagle, while number 41 could be the sighting of a woodchuck at its den, along with corresponding notes of activity. You are limited in your map-coding only by your imagination. It is best for you to design your own method, for that method will make the most sense to you.

CONCLUSION

Project Daytrip for Habitat launches you into the areas that may serve you for years as ecological niches housing the species of your interest. The project also brings about a sub-project, using maps to record when a specific event took place,

Wildwatching can be very relaxing, and a bird like this can be observed close to home.

what species that event pertained to, and exactly where the sighting took place. The daytrip (or bicycle venture for mountain bike enthusiasts) serves as healthy exercise and complete relaxation.

6

Project Signpost

INTRODUCTION

We know that many wild creatures "live by their noses." Project On the Wind was designed to sharpen your own awareness of odors, and at the same time to help you become more sensitive to the fact that many essences rule the behavior of the subjects you want to watch, photograph, and learn about. Having found, through Project Daytrip for Habitat, your own wildlife niches to enjoy, you can now study the movements, actions, and interactions of certain animals. This can be done by building a signpost or scentpost, a scented stopping-off place of interest to various ground-dwelling wildlife. Your signpost may attract birds as well as animals.

One of my signposts became an attraction for a group of ravens, those cousins to the crow. The big black birds would often light near the post and then thoroughly "track up" the immediate area before returning to other interests. Then they lifted skyward with their usual complaints, continuing to caw! caw! long after they were airborne. I don't know why the ravens were so frequently attracted to that signpost, since there was never anything to scavenge around it, but they were.

Depending upon such conditions as temperature, wind, time of day, and other factors, scent may travel quite far on the air currents. Animals may be lured from a considerable distance by signposts. How well signposts (or scentposts) work is addressed below.

OBJECT OF THE PROJECT

There are many means of enjoying wild-watching, but before any wildlife watching

Wild animals, especially quadrupeds, use their noses to guide much of their activity. Wildwatchers can use this fact to lure animals for direct and indirect observation.

can commence, you have to have a subject. You've systematically worked to improve your abilities afield, from upgrading your ability to observe to sensitizing your hearing. You have become much more aware of the scents of animals. You have sought out a good place to enjoy wildwatching and for the most part have located wildlife by slow-pacing through the land. Sometimes, however, you can lure your subjects to you rather than searching them out.

That is the goal of this project, to build a territorial signpost that will attract various wild creatures close in, if not to observe—we can't always be sitting nearby waiting for "someone" to drop in—then to enjoy as an after-study through the vari-

ous sign left behind by the visitor. Later, we'll talk about remote control photography and voice-activated tape recorders that can also be set up around a signpost.

Other objects of this project are to observe animal circuits and to determine patterns of movement. Proof is often lacking in wildlife study; we gain evidence instead of hard facts. When enough evidence is gathered, however, you can develop a defensible scenario. Such a scenario occurred with one of my signposts. By sweeping around it (dusting the area), I was able to record various animal tracks. The signpost was only a few hundred yards from my dooryard, so I had the opportunity of checking it often. For a few months, I noticed a set of tracks belonging to a bobcat. The cat was obviously interested in the signpost; however, he did not visit it daily, or every other day, or even weekly. I named him the "Fortnight Cat," because his visits to the scentpost were gapped quite regularly by ten days. I concluded that the bobcat was on a specific circuit that brought him by my signpost about every ten days.

Another object of the signpost is to learn a lot about a specific animal. While an animal like my Fortnight Cat may be a rather infrequent visitor to the local signpost, other animals may come to the lure on a much more regular basis. This gives you a chance to learn a lot about the behavior of one animal. The world of wildlife is one of personalities. While animals and birds exhibit recordable behavior as a species, each member of the species will also exhibit very unique peculiarities of individual behavior. A group of dump bears came in often, not only to a local dumpsite in northern Arizona, but especially to a scentpost built there. In no time, each bear's personality was evident, from a timid young bore to a short-tempered old she that would take a swipe at anything in her path.

The final object of building a signpost is to aid photography. Recently, two animal types proved much better photography subjects after I set up a signpost for them. One group of these creatures reacted quite normally to the scent and flag attractors. These visitors were pronghorn antelope. I was able to photograph them as they paced around the post a few times, sniffed the scented flag, and soon went about their business of eating, an all-day-long pastime.

The other group, prairie dogs, reacted in an unexpected way to the signpost. They loved to play around the signpost, and through doing so, offered many photographic opportunities. Individual prairie dogs often remained around the scentpost for a half hour or longer before scurrying off to other business.

EQUIPMENT

Little equipment is needed. One object of the scentpost is to attract a wildlife subject, leading to direct observation, an opportunity to study the sign that the subject(s) left around the signpost, or perhaps a chance to capture on film or audio tape an interesting sequence. But don't forget that attraction is not the only reason for a signpost. Holding the interest of the animal is equally important. If the wildlife subject wanders by, stops a second, and then departs, not much observation is allowed. It's still great just to get a look at a passerby, but holding its interest is a lot better.

This requires the type of lure that will not only draw a subject into the signpost, but also hold it there. Commercial scents, nicely packaged in plastic squeeze bottles, are the lures most used today. They are convenient, and they do work. Another lure, ordinary anise oil, can also be very effective. A photographer in Colorado used anise oil to lure black bears for the best sequence of bear photos he ever took.

Another part of the equipment for this project is the signpost itself. Often, it is just a shaft or wood post driven into the ground, but a signpost can be made of almost any natural object in the environment, especially a log, stump, or cluster of rocks. Another scent lure, though often we do not think of it as such, is food. Many different types of foods will lure wild animals in. (More on various foods later in another project.)

An old hunk of log and a couple of scents and you have a signpost.

In the main, however, our lures are composed of bottled natural secretions that attract animals during the estrus cycle. I am convinced that many lures work because of the animal's natural curiosity. There often seems no logical explanation for the behavior of certain signpost visitors, other than curiosity. Why else would a prairie dog have such interest in a scent designed to attract deer?

METHODS AND PROCEDURES

The procedures for this project are simple and straightforward. First, read your area to determine that it is home to the wild animal of interest. You would not, for example, build a signpost for white-tailed deer in a high western mountain setting; however, in the very same vicinity, lower in elevation and along a waterway of some sort, a signpost for whitetails would be appropriate.

It's no secret that "edge," or a change in the landscape, creates habitat for many wild animals. Nobody knows why; however, one good guess has to do with edibles and cover. Edge offers both. There are many types of edge. A good example is a meadow, which provides a definite change in the landscape. The surrounding forest is good cover for wild creatures and serves

Edge like this is a good place to erect a signpost for future observation. Note how the elk are feeding where timber and meadow join.

as home to many different varieties, while the open spaces of the meadow allow penetration of sunlight and the growth of edible browse plants. Edge is also created by a swamp, or a lake, or a marsh — even by streams and rivers. Scentposts along various edge habitat work very well.

Along a section of edge created by a pond with dense cover on one side and a meadow on the other, a signpost I set up had twenty-seven different visitors during a checkup period of thirteen days. These visitors were those I actually saw or those that left clear and definite tracks and/or droppings around the post.

Learn the territory first. Consider the ecological niches and look for terrain alterations that constitute edge. Then decide on a spot and erect a signpost — or simply douse a log, stump, or rockpile with commercial scent or anise oil.

As Realtors say, location isn't everything, it's the only thing. Location makes or breaks the signpost. After looking for ecological niches and edge, take a walk along various trails in the area. A trail can be an excellent place for a signpost. Of course, the post must be erected so you can see it well from a vantage point.

An exception is a signpost that is to serve only to apprise you of mammals in the area. Then an out-of-the-way trail is fine. Check for signs of activity no matter where you intend to erect the signpost, and pay attention to the prevailing direction of the wind before you decide on an exact location for the scentpost.

I realize that last point is obvious, but it's too important to pass by. A signpost is like a room deodorizer, giving off scent to the surrounding area. If, however, you are located between the scentpost and the incoming wildlife, the residents of the locale are going to smell you and shy away from the post. In the morning, cold air lies along the bottomlands, then begins to rise as the day warms. Post yourself high at this time of the day so your scent will not drift into the lower reaches of the area.

In the late afternoon, the situation changes; the cooling air begins to drop down into the lower reaches. Human scent will fall with the lowering air curtain. So you must be aware that if you are seated directly above the signpost as the cool air drifts down to the post, any incoming wildlife may be warned off. Wind changes all this. You need to have the breeze coming from the scentpost to you, not going from you to the scentpost.

You've "read" the area and located the signpost, and you're positioned advantageously in relation to the post—now comes the time to observe, record, and photograph. Patience brings the payoff. I had located a horse that the winter had claimed. That horse was a natural signpost for a number of coyotes in the region. It was two weeks before I saw any, however. The coyotes were observing no particular time pattern. I saw the first two at noon—not in the cold light of early morning or the fading light of sunset, as I had expected, but at midday.

It doesn't matter how good the signpost is or how overrun the area is with wildlife,

Patient observation of the signpost may allow the wildwatcher to observe his subject directly with binoculars or camera. The signpost will also provide indirect observation, as through prints in the soil.

the animals will use the post at their discretion, more often in the early and late parts of the day for some animals, only at night for many predators. Because of this nighttime use, you may wish to "dust" the area for prints. This means sweeping the locale around the scentpost so tracks can be clearly imprinted.

Give the signpost a chance. Your scent lingers about. It may take a few days for wild animals to be drawn by the commercial lure or anise oil and come to the post.

Two last steps to consider—using a flag and setting up for nighttime observation. In the wide-open spaces, a flag tied to a scentpost can lure animals in. The process is simple enough. Tie a piece of cloth to a shaft of wood. (I don't think color matters, but I've always used a white rag.) Douse the cloth itself with lure, then fol-

After dressing the scentpost with liquid lure, dust the area. The earth will then reveal information about any visitors.

low all of the usual procedures in using the scentpost, from overt observation to dusting the site for tracks. A flag blowing in the breeze may prove too much for the curious. I have seen whitetailed deer and antelope move in on a flag and remain long enough at the station to offer plenty of observation time.

As for nighttime observation, a summer evening, especially in a wilderness setting, can offer many thrilling experiences. The two most exciting wildwatch encounters of my life have taken place at a scentpost at night. One was many, many years ago on the Arizona/Mexico border, when my good friend Ted Walter and I were watching by a signpost.

We held our light beam-up that night to illuminate the area with a soft flood of light, without frightening incoming animals. A scream that made us suck in our breaths cut the cool air. We leveled the spotlight on the post and saw probably the only jaguar either of us would ever encounter in our lifetime. The observation did not last long. We were staying in a nearby cabin; we made immediate tracks for the shelter. Twice on the way back, we spotted the cat off to the side of the trail. Jaguar are not supposed to find human fare that tasty, but we didn't want to test the hypothesis.

The other nighttime thriller came in summertime again, in the Colorado high country. I was alone by a beaver pond with a spotlight overlooking a natural signpost, a sheep that had been killed by a bear. The bear moved in on the carcass and picked it up like a dog biscuit. I remained very still and very quiet. My perch was off the ground, but a blackie can climb like a cat, and though nobody gives the little brother of the grizzly much credit for ferocity, there are more documentations of black bears and people mixing than of grizzlies and people, with the people coming off the worse for the encounter.

RECORDABLE OBSERVATIONS

Predators and nonpredators alike respond to signposts. There are many opportunities for recordable observations. When wildlife subjects are lured in by aromas that excite their systems, strange things can happen, although I have never seen a serious skirmish among animals attracted by a scentpost.

Look for interaction of wildlife subjects

A flag can be both a scent and a visual lure. The waving may draw visitors, and the scent may hold the curious animal for a while.

A natural signpost can be a good place to locate wildlife subjects. Even if you don't actually see these subjects, they will leave messages in the earth for you to read.

that are responding to a signpost and record these. Besides your written notes, you may record many interesting sounds at the signpost. The tape recorder offers a means of capturing these sounds while the naturalist is home by the fireside or tucked into bed.

The camera is, of course, another means of freezing scentpost action for later study and enjoyment. But one of the most interesting aspects of signpost observation remains the comparison of data. As you read the works of other naturalists concerning the behavior of wild creatures, see how much of the information matches, or refutes, your own sightings. You may be surprised by both agreements and disagreements in the findings.

CONCLUSION

Patience pays off, as I have said before. However, I promised to speak of the effectiveness of the signpost. Like any other worthwhile endeavor, it won't work every time, but that doesn't make the signpost a second-class project. The stargazer who watches the heavens for special observations of galaxies or locations of planets is not rewarded every night with the wonders of the universe, but he doesn't give up skywatching because meteor showers don't fill the telescope every time he points it skyward. Building a signpost is *one* means of wildwatching and is a project worthy of your time and consideration. The signpost can present a wildlife theater for the observer, and that show is worth waiting for.

7

Project Tape Recorder

INTRODUCTION

A tape recorder and tapes can reveal wonderful facts about wildlife and create some of the most interesting wildlife mementos. Sometimes it takes a little bit of detective work to unravel the meanings of the sounds heard on tapes, and certain sounds will remain forever a mystery. Was that the scream of a hunting bobcat on a distant ridge, or the cry of a bird close to the recorder?

Maybe you'll never know, and I'm not sure that it always matters. The wildworld is alive with interesting sounds, and through the modern technology of the tape recorder we can capture those sounds for our own tape libraries.

OBJECT OF THE PROJECT

The object of this project is to capture on sound tape the many audible communications of the wildworld. Because we now have excellent compact tape recorders at modest cost, anyone can employ the recorder to capture the utterances of wild creatures. Those sounds, incidentally, may emanate from a backyard or from the "forest primeval" far from civilization. Bird feeders are perfect for recording areas, as are springtime nests. But just about any ecological niche where mammals and birds reside will do. I have recorded the springtime chatter of squirrels and the gossiping of prairie dogs in a summer town.

Many interesting tapes are born of backyard adventures; some of ours came during a camping trip. In an out-of-the-way section of Idaho, my family and I spent a week living along a creek. We recorded the booming of partridges, howling of coyotes, even a moose thrashing in a willow thicket.

The tape recorder can capture the sounds of many wild creatures, from the backyard, to the local park, to the wilderness setting.

EQUIPMENT

For daytime recording, where you can leave a recorder and return to the site within an hour or two, the ordinary tape recorder will serve admirably. For nighttime listening, where you may not return to your machine for hours, the voice-activated unit will be more convenient and effective. The latter will, of course, work equally well for daytime listening.

I prefer the compact machine for either day or night and in any setting, from bird feeder to remote mountain pond. The price is reasonable for these models, and they are very portable and adequately sound-sensitive. A battery-operated unit that can switch to either AC or DC at home would sell for $50 to $60. For half that price, you can buy a machine with a built-in equalizer, auto-stop, and belt-clip but sound quality will not be as good.

There are also outdoor models. I have one that cost $25 and is encased in a waterproof plastic shell. I don't recommend leaving this or any recorder in the elements, but I've set the plastic-housed machine out in the morning sun and picked it up following an afternoon cloudburst—wet, but unharmed.

A favorite wildlife recorder of mine is a microcassette unit. This little machine fits in the palm of my hand; it's less than an inch thick. But it picks up nicely, especially around the bird feeder. It is voice-activated, a feature that is handy. It's auto-

Tape recorders, especially voice-activated models, give the wildwatcher a chance to catalogue many interesting sounds of nature. These sounds can be reviewed many times until they "make sense."

You can purchase a windscreen for your microphone or make one from a paper towel tube. Simply insert the microphone into the tube.

stop, functions on AC or DC, and has a built-in mike and a mike jack. Using Micro-90 tape, the machine records for 90 minutes at fast speed or 180 minutes at slow speed.

Although some of the better micro-cassette models sell for about $100, you can purchase a voice-activated model for half that price. The less expensive model is not quite as compact as the more costly unit, but it is still small — under five inches in length and just a bit over an inch thick. It works with batteries or AC adapter. At $50 it's a better buy than a $40 unit I checked that was *not* voice-activated.

There are many standard cassettes that are also voice-activated, and these are the best units for wildlife-listening. They do not offer the convenience of the true compact models, but they are still quite small. And, being voice-activated, there are no silent gaps on the tape with these models. They also have built-in microphones and external mike jacks. A standard cassette, seven inches long, with all of the above features was priced at $60. It worked well in my tests, operating on AC or DC. These recorders all use standard tape cassettes.

I recommend an external microphone for wildlife listening. You can place these remote mikes close to the subject, even in a particularly small space such as near a nest, without the least disturbance to animals or birds. The external mike works far better than trying to conceal a tape recorder nearby. They are not expensive; $5 will buy one and $15 will purchase an omnidirectional unit with a windscreen. The windscreen can be quite important because wind may activate the recorder or distort the sound recorded by the machine. If your external mike is without a windscreen, a slip-on foam unit can be added for under $2. Incidentally, be certain that the mike cord is at least six feet long.

METHODS AND PROCEDURES

Nothing could be simpler. Find the subject or subjects of your interest and place the tape recorder near their activity center. If you place your recorder by an active bird-feeding station, for example, you will, in short order, have an opera of sounds you have never before heard so clearly and distinctly and with such understanding.

A simple roof of wood will protect a tape recorder from the sun. Be sure to enclose the recorder in a plastic bag if rain is possible.

You will want to both hide and protect your tape recorder, so that it will be there when you return for it, safe from the elements, including the sun. A tape recorder blasted by hot sun is endangered, as is the tape within the machine. Secure your machine, turn it on, and walk away.

If the tape recorder is voice-activated, it will turn on only when sufficient sound strikes it. If it's not voice-activated, select the longer tapes, such as 120-minute cassettes, and choose optimum time periods for recording—early morning, late afternoon, and, if possible (for many mammals especially), nighttime. On a campout, it's quite easy at a late hour to place the recorder along a nearby trail or by a stream or pond. Superfluous noises may invade the tape, but that's part of recording wildlife sounds.

The tape recorder can supply a whole library of wildlife sounds. It can be used in conjunction with a written record.

RECORDABLE OBSERVATIONS

If you have an interest in learning what the animals are saying, a tape-recorded session is far better than simply listening. By recording wildlife sounds, you can compare them and learn the meaning of specific repeated sounds. Animals don't often make random noise; their utterances make sense. Even the rumbles of feeding bears have meaning. They may sound like simple guttural pleasure, but listen long enough and patterns will emerge.

Lions may "talk" incessantly as they feed; often, this conversation is a warning to the less powerful of the pride—"Stay away! I'm hungry." Birds have a very complex set of vocal communications.

Although mammals are higher in the animal kingdom, don't expect gibberish from the birds. For a very long time, we've known that bird calls have meaning, usually for marking their territory. Many bird communications are part of the mating ritual and cycle and others are alarm calls. Leave your tape recorder at the bird feeder, and in time an alarm call of one sort or another will be recorded.

Blue jay warnings are common. We were feeding Steller's jays in Arizona one year, and their cries were clearly distinguishable. When the neighbor's cat came around, the jays warned the entire bird community instantly. There was no mistaking the message. We also learned that our jays were frauds. When they wanted the entire feeding area to themselves, they voiced the warning call, even though no enemy was in sight. The area cleared of birds instantly, and the jays moved in undisturbed.

Scientists who study bird language have learned a great deal about their communications. For example, the song sparrow has a danger cry, but it goes further than that—there is one call for aerial danger, another, distinctly different, for ground danger. I once heard sparrows sounding the "danger overhead" alarm, and when I went out, I saw a sparrowhawk diving on the smaller birds. It caught one but couldn't hold it—the sparrow struggled free and took flight. If sparrows can swear, that one was doing it.

There is also a "safe" call, which may follow an alarm call, and you know that the flying hawk or strolling cat kept on going. Mobbing noises can be heard at times. Little birds like to harass big birds— that's mobbing. Sparrows may fly after hawks, owls, ravens, or crows, for example.

You may hear a great deal of song and then silence. That silence generally represents a threat at the feeder. This time the birds don't squawk about it. They freeze, survey the situation, and decide not to voice the alarm call. After you have listened to your tapes a few times, you will be able to interpret these calls.

There are too many distinct sounds to catalogue here—the nightcry of the coyote, the scream of the bobcat, the screech of the owl, the scree! of the hawk, as well as a myriad of intercommunications that pass between birds and animals. Often, an animal will instantly heed the warning call of a bird. There are many special songs around a bird nest when "school is in session" and the youngsters are learning how to speak the language of their parents. And there are yet-to-be interpreted sounds of the wildworld. Perhaps you will record and explain some of these as you expand this project.

CONCLUSION

A tape recorder can be an educational tool. There is, however, another benefit from this project—enjoyment. The sounds of the wild can be as relaxing as music.

8

Project Build a Blind

INTRODUCTION

Great wildlife photographs can be taken from a blind, and valuable wildlife studies can be conducted as well. A blind does much more than conceal you; it also prevents you from being scented or heard by the wildlife you want to photograph and study.

There are many types of blinds — natural, altered natural, and commercial are just a few. Nature provides many strategically located settings that can conceal you. Modest alteration of a natural setting creates another type of blind. Here, you change the landscape a little bit in order to create a blind from the habitat itself. Or you may wish to purchase a ready-made blind. Tree stands are one type; others resemble camouflaged tents. There are also combinations of natural and man-made elements that become excellent blinds.

As you wait in your blind for something interesting to come into view, you must put to use some of the skills you have developed. You must watch and listen attentively. Sometimes your nose will alert you to an incoming subject. And one more thing — blinds offer the physically handicapped person a wonderful way to watch wildlife without having to traverse the countryside.

OBJECT OF THE PROJECT

The object of this project is to employ blinds as one method of wildlife watching. If you use a commercial unit, or recognize natural blinds and know how to use them, or build one of the many other types of concealments discussed here, you add an important and major dimension to your overall wildwatching abilities while in-

Just about any patch of vegetation or a rock formation offers a natural blind. With camouflage paint or a head net, this observer would be very difficult to see.

creasing your enjoyment and knowledge of the outdoors. Here is how.

EQUIPMENT

The tool needed for preparing the blind is a cutting or chopping instrument, such as a portable minisaw or a large, strong-bladed knife. The saw is the safer of the two. A hatchet or hand axe is equally workable and can be kept sheathed until used. These tools help to rearrange the landscape to embellish a natural blind or provide further concealment for any type

of blind, thereby enhancing your chances of seeing your subjects clearly without their detecting your presence.

You should never cut any natural, growing vegetation to build a wildlife blind. I have never known a setting to fail to provide ample blind-making material with dead wood and fallen leaves and tree branches. It harms nothing to cut dead vegetation. If you do not use a natural blind, you will need a commercial blind or tree stand. Or you will need fabric, such as camouflage cloth or cheesecloth, to use as concealment aids in the blind.

METHODS AND PROCEDURES

Erect a blind where the animals are, or if selecting a natural blind, pick one that is located near wildlife habitation and movement. There are many strategic locations for a blind—including the backyard. I have seen endless numbers of bird feeders, birdhouses or birdbaths, and squirrel feeders that offered no concealment for the wildlife watcher. If the naturalist wanted to observe, and especially to photograph, the birds or squirrels, he had to reveal himself—swish! Bird wings whir, squirrel feet scurry, and there's not a single subject left in sight to enjoy. The concept of a blind should be a very broad one. If you have a kitchen window positioned so you can look out into the backyard and photograph through it (without being detected by the visitors there), then you have, for all practical purposes, a blind.

Edge, the transitional terrain previously discussed, is right for the erection of a blind, or a natural "hide," as the British call such concealments. Ponds are excellent sites for blinds, as are water holes. Most watering holes, with the possible exception of backyard "tanks," do not offer a view of the larger mammals in the region. They are excellent for birdwatching, however, as well as for studying amphibians and reptiles. Mammals and some birds, such as the wild turkey, may drink water during the very early morning, late afternoon, and very often at night, especially in arid regions, but they will not drink during the day.

Crossings are good locations for blinds; trails may work well; flyways can be good. Saddles are sometimes busy boulevards for some animals. A saddle is a small area, usually flat, that joins two ridges. Orchards, even country gardens and livestock

Only fallen vegetation is cut for a blind.

feedlots, often make perfect wildwatch locations.

The Natural Blind

The natural blind may be an arrangement of boulders along a trail, or a thicket by a stream, or a blowdown (slash) in edge country, or any number of indigenous obstructions that offer concealment while allowing a view of the surrounding area. There are many such natural hides in the outdoors. I watched a herd of deer in a winter yard without ever erecting a blind, and I wasn't seen once. There was a dry waterway nearby. The bank had been eroded, and it offered a platform to stand on. Standing up, my head just reached above the edge of the ditch and the vegetation concealed my face. That was a good natural blind.

The Altered Natural Blind

Suppose there had been no plants for concealment as I observed the deer yard

A natural blind can be created by simply moving dead foliage around. This hunk of tree trunk will be the basis for a blind along a trail.

above. The first time I poked my head out of the ditch, the deer would have scattered—unless I altered the natural condition of the landscape a little. Use the saw or hand axe to cut *dead* vegetation, and that vegetation will complete the natural blind.

You can "plant" twigs by cutting dead branches at an angle and driving these sharp-ended twigs into the ground as a fence to look through. Or brush can be cut and stacked neatly, with a "lookout hole" left in the pile. A natural blind is altered in another very important way—the area underfoot is cleared for a "floor." This does no damage to the environment, and it prevents boot-scuffling noises and promotes viewer comfort.

A latticework of intertwined vines can also make a nice "window" to look through. This is simply set up as an integral part of the natural blind. An excellent means of making a very good blind from a natural setting is by adding "camo cloth" or cheesecloth. The former is commercial cloth with camouflage patterning; the latter is simple (and cheap) cheesecloth, which may be purchased from a fabric shop.

Camo cloth or cheesecloth can be used to complete a natural blind. Cheesecloth, or any porous material, is stretched and attached between two stakes or branches, then adorned with leaves or twigs for camouflage. Sometimes twigs tear the cloth so I prefer fallen leaves to twigs to dress the

Cheesecloth netting makes a good foundation for a blind.

Add fallen leaves and twigs to the netting to make a good blind. This one is not complete.

cloth. The leaves stick nicely, and even if they don't pull away completely from the cloth when you want to move on, they don't tear the material. The cheesecloth "mask" is very easy to set up, and it's also totally portable, folding into a small package of minimal weight. Camo cloth works the same way, but because it's premarked, no leaves or twigs are needed. The *altered* natural blind makes an excellent hide at a minimum of expense, and it can be structured to suit a specific situation.

The Commercial Blind

Some of the best blinds are commercially made. There are many available at sporting goods shops, especially where camping gear is sold. They add an expense to wildlife watching that is not incurred with the natural blind or the altered natural blind, but no blind works better than a factory model. There are various types of commercial blinds, some with framework, some without. They are portable, generally have a carrying bag, and come in various styles.

One type of commercial blind is the tree stand. This blind puts you above the floor of the habitat and out of sight. A tree stand can be camouflaged with foliage.

The Pit

If you own your own wildlife niche you can dig a pit for observation. It can be as elaborate as a wood-lined underground box with chair and ventilated heater, or as simple as a hole with some sort of concealment about the edges so you can look out while remaining unobserved. Another sort of pit that can conceal you is the natural "hole in the ground," or watercut. There are numerous such depressions in most

locales, and many dry streambeds that will hide you.

The Boat Blind

You can fit boats with covers of various sorts to serve as floating blinds. One such boat had a commercial pop-tent blind altered to fit. These are excellent for photographing waterfowl. Also, many wildlife pictures and observations are available from the water. I once had a chance to watch nesting eagles above a small river. In this instance, we pulled into the brush and used the brush to conceal the topmost part of the boat. The birds soon forgot we were there, and our binoculars provided a living cinema of their activities.

Old Cabins

Where I live, there are many abandoned homesteads with cabins on them. Farms, ranches, and much public property have similar structures. Wildlife has long since grown used to these old buildings, and you can station yourself within one of the enclosures. Be sure to locate a lookout port. I have seen wild creatures from owls to deer around such buildings. For all practical purposes, these old cabins can be thought of as blinds.

Baiting

It is quite legal to bring a bait into many regions while erecting a blind for wildwatching and photography. Such baits can be scents as described in "Project on the Wind," or barnyard livestock that have died. Many wild creatures will come to such baits and can be observed and photographed from the blind. Watch wind direc-

An abandoned cabin or homestead can be useful as a "natural" blind because, to resident wildlife, it has become a part of the landscape.

tion, remain quiet, and you may see some very interesting animals up close and willing to stay put while feeding, sometimes for hours. On the same principle, a blind can be coupled with a scentpost.

The Stalking Screen

I once took a piece of heavy cardboard, large enough to hide behind, and wired dead twigs and brush to it. Then I cut an observation port in the cardboard, and with camera slung around my neck, proceeded to get close to game, especially deer, that were wintering not far from my home. The results were mixed. The greatest warning to wildlife is often motion of any sort, and though the camouflaged screen was no threat when at rest, in motion it became an untrusted thing. The stalking screen *may* prove useful to you in some areas.

This is a bear bait. The heavy barrel contains offal, and there are bits of bait tied to the tree with wire. This sort of scentlure works well in areas with many predators and scavengers.

Camouflage

Camouflage can be a major part of blind-watching. Many natural blinds offer only partial cover. We can improve these blinds by carefully adding dead vegetation to offer a better hide. When on the roam, however, a natural blind can be enhanced when you use camouflage. Hide your hands and face as well as the rest of your body. Too often, wildwatchers in camo outfits are easily detected because the parts of the body that move a lot, hands and faces, are very conspicuous. Use face netting and paint your hands. The idea is to melt into the environment. Rather than trying to hide *behind* brush, for example, nestle *into* the brush. A solid background gives the watcher away because he stands out in contrast to it, rather than blending in.

Watch for reflections, especially from cameras and binoculars. Cameras and binoculars can be dulled with camo tape. Today many binoculars have "built-in" camouflage patterns of their own. Use shadow wisely. Settle down in the shade when possible, because then you are much harder to see. Combining camouflage with a blind is useful, but nothing takes the place of being truly hidden by the blind itself.

Tips for Using the Blind

Even in a blind, especially when blocked only by a screen of brush, you simply must stay fairly still if you want to remain a secret to the wildlife you wish to study. Being quiet is a lot easier when you are comfortable. Clear the blind of debris; if you have a tarp handy, or an old rug, make a floor for your blind. This will be warmer

Paint your hands. Reflection from hands and face can frighten away prospective wildlife subjects.

and quieter than bare ground. In cold weather when you're not moving around, it's difficult to stay warm. Take sufficient clothing; electric socks can help. You can also use a portable heater. Fumes from the heater will be no problem if the wind is in favor of the blind.

Pour masking scent near the blind to counteract the unnatural aromas of the blind (including yours). Carry a plastic drop cloth to ward off rain — it will make a roof for your blind. If you wear a camouflaged face mask, or if you have a camo screen or cheesecloth in front of your blind, ensure that it doesn't wave in the breeze, sending the wrong signals to your subjects.

RECORDABLE OBSERVATIONS

You can keep two types of recordable observations if you are using a blind. One is a record in print; the other is a record in film — the notebook and the camera. You may use a movie camera, a cam-corder, or one of many still-picture cameras. Perhaps the best part of wildwatching from a blind is seeing the natural reaction from birds and mammals. Many valid natural history studies, from squirrels to wolves, have been recorded from a blind.

Blinds can work in just about any environment, even a backyard wildlife garden, where this bird was photographed.

CONCLUSION

Commercial, natural, altered natural, floating, abandoned building — all of these blinds and many others can offer some of the very best wildlife watching.

9

Project Take a Stand

INTRODUCTION

Taking a stand falls between hiking afield to encounter wildlife and operating from a blind. When you take a stand, you move from location to location, stopping awhile in each place, standing or sitting quietly, at least partially concealed, watching and waiting. To standwatch successfully, you must have a plan. The idea is not to simply walk around until a likely spot is located where you can stay put for a while. You must know when, as well as where, to take a stand. The most propitious site is worthless if wildlife is not likely to pass by. Waiting along a deer trail at noon, for example, would be untimely in most regions.

OBJECT OF THE PROJECT

The object of this project is a close encounter with wildlife through staying still rather than walking. Taking a stand is a passive way of getting close to wildlife subjects—in a sense, the opposite of stalking wild animals and birds to study. From a stand, you can watch nests, burrows, trails, saddles, ponds, and many other microhabitats. You can also do circuit standing in which you move in a pre-planned pattern to a specific number of locales, there to stop and watch.

EQUIPMENT

Camouflage is often very helpful on stand. You may camouflage yourself or carry a screen as described in the previous project. The screen can be either predyed or plain, adorned with leaves and other vegetation and used as a visual baffle between wildlife and wildlife watcher.

The right clothing for stalking must also

When you take a stand, you remain motionless and quiet, increasing the odds that wildlife will move in close for study or photography.

be selected, warm clothing in cold weather and quiet clothing anytime. The stand-watch can't be successful if wildlife is fore-warned of your visit before a stand can even be assumed. Naturally, binoculars and camera are essential equipment on the standwatch.

METHODS AND PROCEDURES

To take a stand, situate yourself in a spot that offers a good view of the immediate area. The stand may be located off a trail, at the edge of an opening, near a feeding area, or in any area where wildlife may show up. What do you do on a stand? Observe. What you don't do is move

Proper clothing can make a big difference in taking a stand. This Browning down coat gives the warmth and comfort needed on a cold day.

overtly, for it is this motion that alerts incoming wildlife to your presence.

A circuit-stand makes it easy to keep careful records of wildlife behavior. First, you conduct a habitat search for a region well stocked in the wildlife subject of your interest. After the trail is established, locate exact places along the circuit that are most conducive to taking a stand. Visit these somewhat regularly for best results in gathering comparative data.

I've learned a series of good standing points along a nearby stream bottom. This particular microhabitat lends itself perfectly to the circuit-standing method. In one location, I saw fifty-two whitetailed deer within a two-hour period. The stand was somewhat typical in that it was *above* the likely trail crossing I was watching.

Mammals, including deer, look around much more than they look up. My elevated position proved to be a good watching place. The distance you maintain from the stand to the place you're likely to see wildlife is important, and on this particular stand, I was 100 yards from the crossing. To get closer would have been foolish. I would have lost the advantage of elevation, and my scent would have been at ground level as well.

From 100 yards, the deer literally filled the viewing area of my 10X B&L binocu-

If the wind remains in the wildwatcher's favor, deer such as these may come within frame-filling distance.

lars, and my 35mm camera drew the deer in for frame-filling shots. No animal saw me on that stand; no animal bolted.

I had selected the exact location through a habitat search. The trail I found was loaded with fresh deer tracks, and I discovered three things that prompted the animals to use that trail: There was a favored watering area on one side of the little stream — hundreds of pointed-hoof tracks were pressed into the damp bank there — and on the other side was a cultivated field with plenty of deer sign. In the middle, the typical "whitetail thicket" offered ample cover for the animals. That was one crossing that paid off.

There are many other spots that work well for standwatching. Unsavory as it may sound, a local dumpsite outside of a small mountain village proved a great attraction to myriad wildlife subjects, from ravens to skunks. On two occasions, black bears moved into the bulldozed hole in the ground to shop around for something to eat.

Ponds make excellent wildwatching places for a stand, too. Select the exact standspot that will keep the prevailing wind in your favor. A good stand must conceal you, but it also must allow you to see well in several directions. Animals use trails; they approach ponds most often from specific directions. If you are pondwatching, check for trails to the water site; these trails will help you decide where to stand.

Understand the movement of animals, and your stands will be more productive. The pond trail above is an example of this fact. Another example of stand location is the flyway for birds. In the Southwest I've taken the high ground with binoculars in hand in early morning and early evening. By searching a wide area, I was able to

Understanding the timetable of wild creatures makes taking an intelligent stand more likely. Knowing when this bird would be active determined when to go on stand near his home.

establish a flight pattern for birds. While looking for flyways, I also found roosting sites and feeding areas. Local bird routes mark the travel of waterfowl in a given region. If you know the local pattern of waterfowl, you can take a stand and click the shutter many hundreds of times in a season.

Timing is vital, however, to all standwatching. In one locale, I watched a fox family for an entire summer. Although I checked the den (from about 150 yards' distance) at all times of the day, rarely was there any outside activity at noon. The best time to see mom and kits was in early morning or late afternoon. Anyone foxwatching at noon is fairly well wasting his time. A woodpile fifty feet from a ranch line shack down the road from me has an

Before taking a stand, be sure that your area has wildlife and know the routes taken by that wildlife. This sure sign of both life and lifestyle is a scrape.

identical clock working for it. Go there in early morning or late afternoon and you can build a whole library of rabbit pictures. Forget midday, except in winter. In winter, if it's sunny, the rabbits are often out, catching the warm rays near the woodpile.

A particular yearling moose used a pond for wallowing, feeding, and general standing around, but I saw him only in the dimmest part of the day, early and late, until one afternoon when he came away from his daytime bed early. I snapped his photo as he splashed across the little waterhole, took photos of his big nose sticking out of the alders, and also clicked a few frames as he fed. You won't be a successful wild-watcher without being in tune with the ani-mal's "clock." There are a few creatures that are "out" most of the day, but the majority of wildlife truly lives by the clock.

Fields make good standing points. A stand along the edges of cultivated fields or natural meadows can often produce good results. And there is also the "moving stand." In high mountain terrain, I've had much success with this concept. Use the binocular first, until you find wildlife. Then move into position to *intercept* the subject of your interest.

Deer on a trail tend to stay on a trail. I've watched coyotes working along a little artery without leaving it. Antelope often pick a path and stay to it. You must spot your subjects before they see you, then maneuver into position. When things go well, the end result is a long watch of animal behavior.

Sometimes, several wildwatchers can work together with a drive/stand. This is delicate work. Carefully study a patch of territory, and consider the paths that will most likely be followed by the wildlife in that niche. Then split the group into drivers and standers.

The drivers move through the territory toward those on stand. The noise of the drivers and their scent encourage wildlife to move ahead of the drivers toward the standers who are waiting to observe them. The drivers must proceed with care, however. If they are too exuberant in their efforts, there will be nothing for the people on stand to study. Instead of crashing through the habitat, they must move along very slowly and carefully. Ideally, the animal will not *see* the drivers, but he will know they're there. The animal will not flee from the drivers; he will merely slip away from them, quietly sneaking along.

Meanwhile, the standers should make themselves comfortable in order to stay still. And wait. The wind must be in their

Taking a stand at a corral may insure a look at ravens or crows. If you know which microenvironment belongs with which species, you can choose the niche in the environment that is home to the animal you want to observe.

favor. Otherwise, their scent will drift toward the incoming animals, alerting them of the standers' presence. So, the standers must place themselves with the wind in their faces, not at their backs.

A bobcat quietly slipped out of a thicket after being moved along by drivers. The drive/stand had worked perfectly. The two persons driving zigzagged back and forth through a river bottom thicket, not trying to snap twigs and scrape brush, but rather putting down a ribbon of human scent. They meant to be heard, of course, but not to terrify the bobcat.

The bobcat moved very slowly toward the stand. It was looking back, not frightened, merely moving away from the ap-

proachers. He walked within fifty feet of the stand. In fact, he never did bolt. Even after the clack of the camera shutter, he continued to move slowly away, then disappeared into a jungle of brush.

Feeders of all different kinds make for excellent stands. If you wish to erect a blind by a feeder, that is one thing; the stand is quite another. When you are on stand you are mobile; that is, you move from one place to another, not taking time to pick out a natural blind or alter one.

There are numerous feed areas that attract hundreds of birds and many mammals. You can move among these slowly, taking a stand from time to time. Patience is often the key to wildlife watching and to the successful stand.

RECORDABLE OBSERVATIONS

An important recordable observation is comparative — comparing wildlife behavior over a period of time in one single microhabitat. I found, for example, that antelope assumed the winter posture in an area behind my home on the basis of their biological clock, rather than weather. I cannot say if this is factual for pronghorns everywhere; however, even when there was no snow, no cold, no climatic indication of winter, the herd formed by several smaller groups joining into one large group. This I learned from one stand only, on a high point overlooking two ponds in a valley.

Your notebook will be replete with information gathered on stand. Of course, wildlife can also be captured on film from a stand. Since you are not in motion, you will have many excellent photo opportunities as you do from a blind. The difference is your mobility. Taking a stand requires no special field time, other than hiking to the spot and assuming a watchful and favor-

Take a stand for burrowing animals. When the animal goes down his tunnel, stand by. Wait him out. He may return, as this prairie dog did.

able position, with the wind coming from the most likely section of the land toward you.

CONCLUSION

The stand offers one more viable means of watching and photographing wildlife. Stands allow a contemplative, relaxed enjoyment of wildlife and the outdoors.

Standwatching is more than merely walking around and then staying still for a while, however. To be successful a stand must be used with *specific* habitat features, such as waterways, trails, fields, and many other microhabitats, and *specific timing* must be employed. The stand serves a double purpose — close positive encounters with wildlife and a quality outdoor experience.

10

Project Birdhouse and Feeder

INTRODUCTION

To fully cover the subject of birdhousing and feeding would require a huge book. There are thousands of different birds with numerous lifestyles, as well as hundreds of various foods and feeding patterns. There are seed crackers and aerial insect-catchers, ground feeders and high feeders. Bird species are as individual as human cultures.

A few years ago I wanted to encourage the beautiful Say's phoebes flying around my home to raise a family on the premises. The birds often hovered at the kitchen window, looking inside for long periods of time, as if they were curious about us.

They obviously were not afraid of our movements, so I decided to erect a fine little birdhouse for them. They never went near the place. They liked the surroundings, however, and raised a family on the grounds, using our upper windowsill as a nesting site. The birds glued the nest to the wooden sill, and it withstood the strong springtime breezes.

The phoebes have returned annually to nest, always on the window platform. I didn't know enough about birdhousing at the time to realize that a shelf-nesting species wouldn't go near the claustrophobic castle I had built, while a cavity-dweller would have been perfectly at home in it.

Placement of birdhouses and feeders is important. Ground feeders may never eat on high-rise platforms, and birds used to finding food in the upper reaches of the environs may never touch the meals you provide for them on the ground in your backyard. We are blessed, however, with a multitude of books dealing with most of our backyard winged visitors. These specific guides can give you first-time success.

At little expense and virtually no travel, you can enjoy an arena of activity on your own grounds if you feed and house birds. Every spring, we follow the family activities of our phoebes, from nestmaking to rearing the young. Finally, the cycle is completed. The young birds are diving on insects like World War I biplanes, while the parents watch from a rooftop vantage point.

This project is a get-started venture. It will launch one of the most interesting aspects of wildlife watching—observing birds and squirrels in the backyard. Many naturalists try at first to shoo away the squirrels that come to the bird feeder for a free meal. After a while, because the clowns of the treetops are so enjoyable to watch, they are as welcome as the winged visitors.

Housing and feeding birds can be ABC simple, or it can be as complex as you desire. There is no doubt that birdhouses and feeders liven up a backyard. They also serve as teaching posts. Watch long enough, and the birds, along with other wild and domestic creatures, will teach you something new. You can learn about the territorial imperative, the meaning of avian songs, nesting practices, feeding

This rock, dished out by the elements, made an excellent feeder. Note the cracked seeds. A simple bird feeder can relay much information to the wildlife watcher.

practices, the rearing of young (who take flying lessons as well as singing lessons from their parents), and many other facets of behavior.

Backyard birdwatching has produced many important and interesting findings over the years. The phenomenon of anting was first noted by Audubon in 1830; however, many modern ornithologists studying in the backyard setting have added numerous notations concerning this. It took close observation for the naturalist to realize what anting birds are really doing. Birds deliberately stand either directly on an anthill or in a line of ants, allowing the little insects to crawl through their feathers. Sometimes birds seize individual ants in their beaks, preening their feathers with the juices of the insect. The formic acid from the ants (and the insect bites as well?) may have a therapeutic effect on the anting bird. Backyard birdwatching helped to bring the process of anting to light.

Wildlife watching at the birdhouse is far more than merely getting a good look at the bird population. Here is how to get started.

OBJECT OF THE PROJECT

The object of this project is to *attract* and to *enjoy* birds, as well as incidental mammals, and to offer an opportunity to learn about these creatures without having to venture from the backyard. There is, perhaps, a more noble reason for inviting birds to your "lunch counter." The habitat has changed. Wildlife needs four survival entities: food, water, shelter, and space or "cover." Shelter and space have shrunk in our technosociety. Food for birds and other wildlife has also diminished significantly. I have seen fifty pounds of birdseed disappear in a week of bird feeding in a residential backyard.

Such heavy use is not only because birds enjoy finding an easy meal; the birds are also coming to dine because they cannot always find enough food in the natural sector. This is especially true for those species that winter in the snowbelt.

Migratory species, such as many of the warblers, will not remain long in your backyard, not even for free room and board. Their goal is wintering in Central America. Even these travelers will linger longer at your homesite, however, if you offer them shelter and food.

EQUIPMENT

Good bird feeders are available in numerous styles. A book on birdwatching will usually include many models at modest prices, suited for various birds under numerous feeding conditions. Bird feeding can be as easy as scattering seeds on the ground, drilling holes in a fence post as cavities for suet, or using a simple table to hold feed. Commercial feeders work well.

A store-purchased feeding shelf works very well for many species of backyard birds. You may have to add a roof to keep rain and/or snow from spoiling the feed. It rains little in my area, so I have an uncovered summer feeding table, an old reel spool (quite large) that was used to hold heavy-gauge wire. It works admirably well. If a feeder is placed on a pole, it can be squirrel-proofed, if you wish, with an inverted metal cone. The squirrels climb to that point but cannot get past the metal barrier.

The aerial feeder also serves to keep squirrels out of the feed. But I like squirrels and they are welcome to some food. So are sparrows. However, I do sympathize with wildlife watchers who are faced with feeding hundreds of sparrows. These little birds, really weaver finches, can be a problem. One way to uninvite them is to supply feeding stations with food that is not their favorite fare.

Birdfood can be very expensive when purchased in small quantities. Feed stores offer seed in large quantities at reasonable prices. One good preparation is millet and sunflower seeds. Many birds, such as evening grosbeaks, juncos, house finches, goldfinches, and others, like this combination. A combination of millet and cracked corn, along with a few sunflower seeds, makes another good birdfood.

I cannot suggest the right feed for your area, because I don't know which birds visit your backyard. Consult a guide and feed accordingly.

Commercial birdhouses do not always work as well as commercial feeders. A specific type of nester has specific needs in a birdhouse. Therefore, a generic birdhouse won't do, whereas a generic feeder may. There are many kinds of bird shelters easily constructed with a few simple tools and economical supplies. Some of the very best birdhouses are constructed in the home shop.

Be sure you know what to build, though. The wrong kind of birdhouse is good for one of two things: nothing at all or one season only. I built not one but three incorrect birdhouses before coming on Alan Pistorius's book, *The Country Journal Book of Birding and Bird Attraction*. My next birdhouse was a pip.

There are so many different types of birdhouses that you should consult a guide before deciding on a style to match your specific bird visitors. Various species require different sizes and styles. A chart showing proper birdhouse sizes and shapes for different species can be found on page 198 of the Pistorius book. Here are some general guidelines. Build your birdhouse with wood. Wood is inexpensive and easy to work with and has reasonably good self-insulation qualities. Furthermore, wood birdhouses are nonconductive; the occupants won't be sizzled in a lightning storm.

Many woods work well for birdhouses. I've used western red cedar with success. White cedar is also good, as is redwood. Use a wood that does not require paint, which isn't necessary on a birdhouse. Buy the "cheaper cuts" of wood; they work fine. Use three-fourths-inch thickness. Thinner wood warps too easily in the elements, and thicker wood isn't needed. This is a house, not a wild animal cage. Rustproof nails are all right, but I much prefer brass screws.

Here is a sample birdhouse I made for cavity nesters. Primary cavity nesters are mainly woodpeckers, birds that drill out their own houses, usually in trees. Secondary cavity nesters, such as wood ducks and owls, are those birds that take over such dwellings after they've been abandoned by primary drillers.

No perch is necessary. A perch will only encourage sparrows to "hang around" this abode. Select rough-cut timber, and be certain that the rough wood is used for the *inside* of the house. This is important because the cavity-type birdhouse has but a small opening high on the front panel. The birds dwell well below in the compartment, and the rough interior walls allow them to easily climb upward to the entrance/exit.

The shape of this birdhouse is boxlike with a roof slanting forward. That's about it. If you're not a woodworker, build your first house of cardboard. The cardboard pieces will be your templates. Cut the six panels of cardboard and fit them together with cellophane tape—floor, four walls and ceiling. When the cardboard house looks right with proper fit, take it apart. Place the cardboard pieces on the wood and trace around each piece.

These cardboard templates will become a simple bird shelter and feeder. The novice woodworker is advised to work with templates.

Be certain that the grain of the wood on the roof runs up and down, so when the wood weathers, the normal grooves, cracks, and checks run "lengthwise" with the house, acting as natural gutters to allow rain runoff.

Saw the six panels of wood out of your stock. Before putting the parts together, drill quarter-inch airholes on the two side panels close to roof level where they are protected from rain by the overhanging roof. Drill similar drainholes in the floor — a couple in the center and one at each corner.

Cut a round hole in the front panel —

centered, and just below the roof level. This is the entrance/exit hole for the house. Drill screw holes through the rear panel and into the two side panels; insert screws through these holes to attach the rear panel to the side panels. Attach the floor and the roof in the same manner. Use sufficient screws to bond the sections of the birdhouse firmly together. In the front panel, however, use only three screws, one dead center just above the entrance hole and one on either side toward the bottom corners of the front panel. This allows you to remove the front panel with a screwdriver. The birdhouse will eventually be-

The cardboard templates are attached with cellophane tape to form the bird shelter/feeder. Refinements can be made. Then the templates will be traced on wood. The wood is cut out and fitted together to form a real bird shelter/feeder.

come filled with debris and useless as a dwelling, but by removing the front panel, you can clean it and return it to like-new condition.

METHODS AND PROCEDURES

Methods and procedures include proper location and application of feeder and birdhouse. I advise a satellite feeding program. This means more than one feeder with more than one type of food in your backyard. Ground feeders can be fed by spreading seed directly on the ground. Use a cardboard pallet if your grass is high, or clear a small area near a bush and scatter seeds there. A bush overhang often gives security to ground feeders that fear hawk attacks from overhead.

You may also want a feeding platform in another part of the yard. Your "English sparrows" may enjoy a mixture of commercial feed with a lot of white millet in it. Add bread crumbs from time to time.

Evening grosbeaks like black-striped and black oil sunflower seeds, which can be purchased in large quantities (fifty-pound bags) or bought from a local farmer's sunflower crop. If you buy from a farmer, be certain that a pesticide was not recently applied. It could harm your birds. In another portion of the yard, toss out a bit of ear corn if you have squirrels. This offering may help keep the bushytails out of the birdfood.

Don't forget that there are many bird visitors, such as jays, that prefer more "meaty" diets. These birds enjoy suet. Suet is *interior* fatty tissue, such as found around the kidney and loin area of beef cattle, not the fat cut away from a porterhouse steak. It is inexpensively purchased from your butcher.

Woodpeckers, chickadees, nuthatches, as well as the jays, will stop by often for a suet treat. Feed by taking a wooden post and drilling holes in it. Poke the suet into these holes, or tie pieces of suet on backyard tree limbs. Grease-soaked stale bread works well in cold-weather feeding, too, for it "sets up" when cold to become quite solid.

Don't turn your feeders into cat traps. If you feed birds, you have to do so protectively. Don't set up the feeders so that the

Don't turn your feeders into bird traps. The neighborhood cat soon learns when a feeder will provide him with an easy catch.

local tomcat can set up an ambush. My feeding table, for example, is cat-proof, as are most aerial feeders if properly suspended. A cat cannot leap from directly beneath my feeding table, because it will encounter only the bottom of the table, and if it attempts to jump up on the table from an angle, it will be seen by any and all feeding birds before it can leap on them.

As for the birdhouse, remember that birds are quite territorial. Certain species (such as martins) are gregarious, and multiple dwellings are fine for them. Many other birds, however, will not nest in close proximity to their brothers. It is wise to place only one birdhouse in your backyard under these circumstances.

I don't believe that absolutely specific birdhouse locations need be observed; but remember that each bird has a preferred location that it finds natural to dwell or nest in. Trying to coax that bird away from its natural habitation is generally pointless.

If your property has fence posts, consider building houses integral with them to

Don't forget that some birds enjoy suet. This suspended cage holds suet and it serves as an ideal feeder.

serve the cavity-nesters. If you have any of the ground nesters nearby, such as many of the quail, you may provide a bit of cover as a nesting site. And if you want to do a lot for birdhousing on your own property, leave trees standing when possible instead of cutting them down. A tree offers a natural nesting site for many birds, is a perfect location for the manmade birdhouse, and plays host to a tremendous food supply for insect-eating birds. If your trees are already gone, or were never there in the first place, build birdhouses.

RECORDABLE OBSERVATIONS

Birdhouses and feeders attract and hold birds for observation. Many birders have a lifelist on which they check off all the birds sighted in the birdwatcher's lifetime. The backyard birdhouse and feeder, simple and close to home as they are, offer excellent opportunities for lifelisters. A ledger, or list of species sighted, can be very interesting and rewarding, and if the whole family works on the birdlist together, it gives the family a chance to interact on a mutual project. Besides simply listing the names of birds sighted, there are numerous other observable recordings to be made at a backyard feeder or birdhouse. Interaction among birds and mammals, not only with their own species but with others, constitute major recordable events. Backyard squirrel behavior alone could fill a notebook.

Birds may be quite territorial and somewhat set in their routine. This one could be found like clockwork on the window ledge in the dim light of early morning.

This very simple feeder beneath a kitchen window can provide hours of birdwatching.

Over a period of two years, a neighborhood cat set about to invade a setup of satellite bird feeders and birdhouses. I doubt that an experiment in feline behavior could have been set up any better as this cat worked at various tricks in an attempt to ambush the visiting birds.

Initially, the cat took the most direct routes including long and impossible leaps into the air that brought nothing but frustration. Later, she tried climbing the feeder post. That worked no better. One day, however, she figured out a new method of reaching the bird feeder. She again climbed the post, but this time she leaped at an

Interactions of birds at the feeder can make for some interesting studies. These two are sharing the same food, but they are distinctly different birds.

angle when midway up the post, her claws grasping at the edges of the feeding platform. She almost made it. I knew that in time she would, so I fitted the post with an inverted metal cone.

The birds' interaction with the cat was as interesting as the cat's methods of trying to solve her problem of reaching the birds. Initially, they flew furiously from the feeding platform at first sighting of the cat. Later on, they discovered that her frantic jumping into the air was meaningless. They fed on as the cat leaped harmlessly into space.

Trying to gauge the mental capacity and communicative abilities of wild animals is no easy matter. While the backyard birdhouse and feeder may not answer questions of intelligence, communication, and behavior traits, the arena serves to teach a great deal, much of which can be recorded for later reference.

The tape recorder offers another means of recording information at the birdhouse or bird feeder. Initially, a tape recorder placed near either feeder or house may cause suspicion, but in time the birds get used to it. It can be camouflaged with leaves or burlap, so that it does not stand out boldly, and it can also be hidden

Although it may be necessary to camouflage a tape recorder, setting one out in the open as glaringly as this one, directly below a simple commercial feeder, may work well.

Building a bird feeder is enjoyable, with great rewards for the wildlife watcher.

among the foliage near a ground-feeding station. Bird songs around a feeder are easily captured, especially with the voice-activated recorder.

CONCLUSION

Project birdhouse and bird feeder is a no-travel adventure requiring little outlay of funds for a large and varied reward. You may observe and record bird and mammal behavior without leaving home. You will realize the enjoyment of bringing wildlife into the backyard and have an opportunity to help supply two of the four major criteria of survival—food and shelter.

The cycle of life continues around the backyard on an annual basis. Every area of the country offers opportunities for bird feeding, birdhousing, and birdwatching. The birds of my immediate area—Steller's jay, Gray jay (camp robber), evening grosbeak, mountain chickadee—probably won't be the same as those found in your area, but yours will be just as interesting.

11

Project Nestwatch

INTRODUCTION

Window bird feeders initiated our nesting-bird watching. The little hummingbirds that came to the window to drink the nectar we provided were entertaining to watch, but it was another feeder, no more than a shelf, that prompted Project Nestwatch. The birds became comfortable with the shelf because they detected our images only as shadows on a frosted pane of window glass.

Then one day a perceptive daughter pointed out that a little bit of construction was taking place on the feeding ledge. The ledge, as it turned out, became a nest. Its location was our good fortune. We had a perfect view of the entire nesting process and rearing of the nestlings. Its only drawback was photographic—the frosted window would not allow a clear picture of our guests. Otherwise, Project Nestwatch was perfect. That first nestwatch led to many others.

Human dwellings lure many nesting birds. They house themselves not only in the homes we provide for them, as noted in the last chapter, but also in drain pipes; chimneys; upon window ledges; and in tool sheds, gutters, and any other crack, crevice, or hole. While our homes and grounds serve as nesting sites for birds, they also serve as blinds for us.

OBJECT OF THE PROJECT

The object of this project is to observe the birdnesting phenomenon without disturbing either parent or nestling. Nestwatching is an art. You must be clever enough to position either the nesting site (when encouraging birds to nest in your backyard) or yourself so that the nest can

Birds have learned to make nests wherever man lives. This grocery store sign provided a nice shelter for a nest.

be watched without the birds being aware of your presence. If you develop the art, you will see courting, mating, nest building, incubation of eggs, hatching of young, feeding of nestlings, development of fledglings, the teaching of the young birds, and finally their departure from the nest.

EQUIPMENT

Man-made nesting sites work supremely well. Therefore, you may wish to include as part of the equipment for this project a nesting shelf or a birdhouse. There are myriad books devoted to the proper build-

ing of bird nests. Novice nest-makers forget that setting up housekeeping for birds is much more than simply supplying a home; you must match the house to the residents.

Phoebes and robins will often nest on a shelf. The nesting shelf is considered here as a tool of nestwatching. A backboard with two sides, a base, and a roof make a nesting shelf. It is that simple. Dimensions vary widely. A successful nesting shelf I built for a family of phoebes had a rectangular backboard nine inches wide and thirteen inches high, with side panels, roof, and base to match these dimensions. The nesting shelf, remember, is for birds that prefer the open area nest site, quite the opposite from cavity dwellers. Therefore, don't be concerned about the spare design of this nesting platform with its totally open front; and remember, if you can place this little structure near a window, all the better for your nestwatching activities.

The idea of nestwatching is to observe the actions and interactions of the birds. At best, the enclosed nesting site, such as a birdhouse, allows you to observe the coming and going of the parents, and later the emergence of the feathered young, but little in between. By all means, provide nesting birds on your property with the correct type of house. For this project, however, consider a nesting platform; it offers a "view." Incidentally, the largest nesting platform I've seen was built for a pair of eagles, a lofty wooden pallet placed in a high tree along a riverbank in the Northwest.

Don't forget optical aids in nestwatching. A telescope allowed us close observation of a white-winged dove nest in Arizona one year, without the parents ever suspecting us. We were invisible to them the whole time. Looking through the telescope, we were able to see the entire nest larger than life, and yet the distance from window to nest site was forty yards or more.

Attach the telescope to a tripod and aim it toward the nest. When you want to check the activities of the nest, simply put your eye to the lens and enjoy the view. Binoculars are better suited to other nestwatching situations where the telescope is not workable.

The camera is another obvious tool of nestwatching. A telephoto lens is a must, for it allows the same sort of nonencroachment enjoyed by the terrestrial telescope and the binocular. The camera may be

mounted on a tripod in a semipermanent location, such as pointing out of a window, throughout the entire nesting period. If the view through the eyepiece is interesting, a simple snap of the shutter freezes the action forever.

METHODS AND PROCEDURES

Invite birds to nest naturally by attracting them to your backyard with proper nesting foliage. Hedges are right for some birds; crotches in trees serve for others. If a tree crotch is cluttered with small branches that make nesting impossible, trim the tangle out of the way so the birds can build. Robins may nest there after you make the site hospitable.

Outbuildings make excellent nesting

A major objective of Project Nestwatch is nestwatching without disturbing the young. Such disturbance can be more than annoying to nesting birds; it may cause them to abandon the nest. These nestlings were photographed from a distance with a strong telephoto lens. They were not disturbed.

sites, too, and are often good for watching. An old tool shed with shelves provides many surfaces for nesters. Once the nests are built and the birds are comfortable, you can watch their progress from time to time by viewing with binoculars. Get too close, and you may send the birds on their way.

Levels of tolerance vary among nesting birds. A local nestwatching friend opened and closed the door of his homemade birdhouse several times during the nesting cycle without pushing the birds away. I recall nesting doves, however, that gave up their eggs after being disturbed by well-meaning neighbors who, every day, had to

see how the eggs were coming along. Nest abandonment after human tampering is not uncommon. Incidentally, tampering can take place during nest-making as well as during egg incubation or the nestling-nurturing period. Poke around the platform where birds are trying to construct a nursery, and they may go on strike.

In a farm outbuilding located in a field, I located the nest of owls. They had, typically, built their nest on a shelf. The birds were disturbed easily, and the only worthwhile nestwatching occurred from a distance and only when the early morning sun was just right, lighting one of the nests well enough to allow a clear binocular view.

Outbuildings make excellent nesting sites. This great horned owl nest is located in an abandoned building.

Still, the watch was entertaining and enjoyable. When the owlets were quite large, their parents fed them whole mice. The "pufflings," as one young observer called the fluffy nestlings, closed their eyes as they worked to engorge the entire mouse from head to tail.

If there is no shelf in your outbuilding, consider making one or several. If an old shed has no particular value, drill holes in it for bird entryways and exits. Place the holes high enough on the side of the structure to discourage easy entry of rodents.

A beginning procedure for the nestwatcher is to provide nesting materials in the area to encourage prospective parents. Certainly, the natural world is filled with such building material; however, it never hurts to lay out a few items to help the cause. Do not place these items on the nesting platform, and above all, never set them inside a nesting box. If you do, the birds may think the area is already claimed. They will move on, and your nestwatch will come to an end before it begins. Place nestmaking materials nearby, generally on the ground, but also in bushes. String, an old straw broom (some birds love this material), cotton balls, narrow strips of cloth, thread, yarn; any of these materials work well for nestbuilding.

Location is very important when picking a site for the man-made nest. The man-made nest should meet the same criteria that natural nesting fulfills: protection from enemies and shelter from the elements. When choosing a place to encourage nest building, keep these features in mind. Do not expect birds to build their nests where they will be exposed to hot sun or direct wind. (Our phoebes elected to build a nest in the windiest place on our home, however, a kitchen window ledge facing the prevailing zephyrs.)

Providing nesting materials is helpful to some birds. Horsehair wound around this tree offered nesting birds a good building material.

Location requirements also include safety from above and below — hawks from on high, housecats from the ground. Rats can be a problem in some areas; so can squirrels and skunks. One wildlife watcher found that his ground nesting birds never did raise a brood successfully; raccoons got the eggs. He elevated a platform over the natural nesting site and fitted it with outreaching fans of tin. The birds took to the slightly elevated foundation and reared their young successfully.

You may be able to encourage birds to build a nest on a window ledge by drawing the window shade and placing food on the ledge. Consider that location as prime. I have found that a clear windowpane within full view of the interior of the house is not very workable, but your birds may not mind the fishbowl lack of privacy. On

Don't forget ground nesting birds. Provide a safe area in your personal environment for ground nesters if possible.

Telephoto lenses aid in recording bird nesting activities without disturbing either parents or young.

the other hand, a frosted pane precludes photography and obscures nestwatching.

I have considered a one-way glass; however, birds would see themselves in this and very likely retreat or attack, perhaps becoming injured on the glass. If you posted a picture of a hawk on this one-way glass, it would serve to save the birds from flying into the window, but it would also send them to another nesting site in a hurry.

Don't forget ground-nesting birds. Encourage ground nesters by offering cleared areas in your yard that are not surrounded by cat-hiding shrubs. A nighthawk built a nest within view of my home one year. I found out only by walking too close to the nest one morning. There was no nest-watching possible that time, but next season and in later years I watched for nesting activity and with binoculars was treated to a fairly good view of a ground nest.

If you own considerable ground, consider ground nesters such as pheasants. Offering feed at ground level may attract them. Two ranching friends of mine have created habitat for pheasants around their large yards. They both had to catproof (and in one case dogproof) the nesting sites, and they both used woodpile methods to ward off hawks, but the pheasants did nest and they did stay. One frosty morning as I was having breakfast with one rancher, a couple of birds walked out onto his snow-covered backyard. The birds were interesting to observe during mating and nesting time, as well as being decorative.

Many birds nest naturally in a backyard that has the proper bushes for it. Usually, this means a hedgerow. Where I lived in the Southwest, our large yard had another kind of plant that proved perfect for nestwatching, jumping cactus. A cactus wren set up housekeeping in one of our spiny plants and gave us the single best nestwatch of all. I think the nesting birds carried on with total naturalness because we never approached the nest site.

RECORDABLE OBSERVATIONS

Project Nestwatch takes in an entire series of activities, from courting to the fly-away of the adolescent birds. All of these activities include interactions of many kinds—parent with parent; parent with nest, egg, and nestling; and parents with intruders, including other birds. You will also see what can amount to very interesting schooling sessions for the fledglings as they learn to mimic the adults. Because the bird's life cycle is compact the nestwatching project allows the recording of a

Make your nestlings safe if you can. Don't provide a nesting site that is going to be raided by other creatures. The busy squirrel will often make a meal of birds' eggs.

complete behavioral cycle in a very short period of time.

You are again urged to record data in notebooks and to build celluloid libraries with 35mm slides, black and white prints, or moving pictures. The tape recorder is an asset to the nestwatch, too. The conversations carried on during nesting time from adult to adult, as well as adult bird to youngster, can be interesting and at times puzzling. The tape recorder captures many variations in "bird talk." When patterns in this avian language are established, records become educational.

CONCLUSION

Nestwatching is a near-to-home activity that requires no expensive or special equipment. It is a learning experience enjoyed by child and adult alike, and it can culminate in the recording of observations that are enlightening as well as entertaining.

12

Project Burrow Watch

INTRODUCTION

Many interesting wild animals reside in burrows—some are nocturnal, others prefer the daytime. Because of their peculiar lifestyles, burrowing animals have their own brand of behavior. There are numerous observable and recordable facets of these lifestyles, rendering Project Burrow Watch extremely worthwhile. Children, especially, gain a great deal from the burrow watch. It teaches patience, and you do need patience for this project. Burrow watching also teaches keen and accurate observation practices. Many of our burrowing wildlife friends show a multitude of interactions and patterns to watch and record.

Although I have had fairly wide experience with badgers, a burrowing animal that is often nocturnal in nature but that lives by day in some of the remote areas I

enjoy, the majority of my current burrow watching is in a prairie dog town. There is a small one within walking distance of my home and a large one on a ranch fifteen minutes away. I've learned a lot about these interesting rodents by observing them from a distance. The occupants of the towns go about their business in a natural way because they do not see me.

Prairie dogs and badgers are just two of the many burrowing creatures. There are even feathered underground den dwellers in my area—burrowing owls. Gophers, mice, shrews, skunks, woodchucks, rockchucks, moles, ground squirrels, many species of snakes—the list goes on and on. Even foxes and coyotes rear young and often reside in cavernous earthen dwellings.

One of the best ways to enjoy burrow watching is to first research a given animal

The prairie dog is only one of many burrowing-type animals. It is a diurnal creature and can be enjoyed during the daytime during good weather.

through the myriad natural history books on the subject, thus making a profile of its lifestyle, and then study that lifestyle through your personal burrow watching observations.

OBJECT OF THE PROJECT

The object of this project is to locate an interesting burrowing species and through a series of specific observations gather data and/or photographs of the animal or animals. I say animal because most burrowers of our particular interest are mammals. Birds, snakes, amphibians, and other underground dwellers are interesting

but not always readily available for study, certainly not in the "out-and-about" manner of a woodchuck. Generally, burrowers of one kind or another can be found close to home, from east to west coast America, and they are not difficult to locate.

There are many activities to observe in burrow watching, including the interactions of animals, their territorial directives, signals of warning, feeding patterns, various means of communicating their demands (including fighting), and many other behavioral traits. Trying to figure out what makes them tick and what their motives are for each action and interaction is intriguing.

EQUIPMENT

You will need a notebook, binocular, telescope, and camera for Project Burrow Watch. The telescope is an especially valuable tool because it allows long-range viewing without disturbing the subject or subjects. The whole idea is to observe the animal's behavioral patterns in its natural state.

Consider a car window mount for the spotting scope (the Bushnell Optical Company makes one). Attached, the mount allows viewing from your car, and many burrow watch candidates live along roadways. Drive slowly until you spot your subject, then pull to the side of the road for further observation. Woodchucks, prairie dogs, marmots, and other burrow dwellers seldom dive into their tunnels or rock entrances at the sight of a vehicle. Should the animal disappear into its burrow, a little patience usually serves to "wait 'em out."

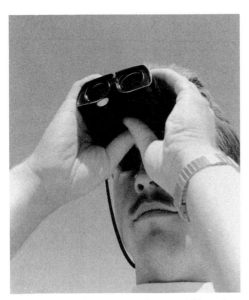

Burrow study often requires the use of binoculars. Here, a compact binocular serves the purpose, a 7X Bausch & Lomb model.

A fox family living in an earthen den behaved exactly in this way. Used to vehicles, yet shy, the mother would usher her kits into the den at the approach of a car or truck. But in moments, the family would be back out, playing, hunting, and learning. The spotting scope attached to a window mount created a close-up view of the action.

Notebook, camera, binoculars, telescope, window mount (a shovel sometimes, as well as an old straw broom) and one other possible tool serve this project admirably. That last tool is a blind. Project Build a Blind covered the details. In burrow watching, the blind is arranged near a den site or other earthen dwelling.

METHODS AND PROCEDURES

The young wildlife lover may gain a great deal from excavating a hunk of earth. No lasting damage is done; disrupted ants soon return to their routine. Meanwhile, your youngster may uncover many special kinds of earth-dwelling creatures from termites to grubs and worms, not to mention tunnelings of various sizes and extents. This is a simple procedure, requiring nothing more than a shovel, although the young observer may wish to retain in a jar a few unearthed treasures.

Caves are another type of den you will find very interesting. I suggest that novice cave explorers stick with the established cave tour or go with knowledgeable and experienced guides. The cave has been a point of wildlife study, especially of bats, for many decades. These winged mammals have proved to be very interesting not only in lifestyle, but also in physiological ability—they are the kings of radar, for example. Caves may present evidence of life that a wildlife detective may enjoy piecing together.

Burrows are generally easy to locate. When their residents are nocturnal, indirect study (dusting, for example) provides information. Direct observation, however, is a problem because the animals are out of sight.

Burrows are usually quite easy to locate. The burrows of many creatures are built in or under a rockpile. Hoary marmots— rockchucks—enjoy this sort of lifestyle. Cottontail rabbits often live in burrows, too, and sometimes these caverns are associated with rock formations. Look for burrows around rockpiles and in banks of earth. I've located many burrows of various kinds along canal banks. One such burrow, home to a bobcat, had been opened into cavern proportions. Chances of seeing the cat at home were very slim. The many bones scattered around the entryway of the den, however, were interesting clues to the animal's activities.

Sometimes the viewer does not actually see his subjects first-hand; he has to enjoy a burrow watch passively, rather than actively. The first step in this kind of study is

to locate an active burrow. Spiders often string webs across the opening of abandoned burrows; an active burrow will be clear of these. In the dirt near the entryway of the burrow there will be fresh tracks and often evidence of past meals. There may also be droppings. A very good test of the active burrow is a dusting. Use an old broom to sweep the entrance area clear. The swept ground will reveal the tracks of all who later visit the burrow, creating a story in the earth to be read by the wildlife watcher.

Dusting a burrow site leads to another method of enjoying the burrow watch— tracking in a circle around the burrow. After dusting the site and picking up fresh tracks at the entrance, try to follow the tracks as far as possible. Oftentimes, the tracks will lead to a trail. A dusted badger

Dust the area in order to determine the current occupancy of a burrow. Fresh earth often entices wildlife, of course, so be certain that the tracks you see in the brushed ground are from the burrow dweller itself and not a passerby.

den revealed the activity of the animal very well. I followed the fresh tracks beyond the burrow and onto a trail. The trail led directly over a hill, down into a little depression, and up again onto a huge tabletop of land—a prairie dog village. The badger made many visits to that village, as evidenced by the path he had worn from his earthen den.

Returns to the badger den found the fellow at home several times. Once, he was hard at work clearing his den. Through the telescope there was nothing visible but a rising spray of dirt. And then the backside of the animal edged out of the hole, feet working rapidly to displace dirt from the den.

There are stories from the pioneer days of the Golden West that tell of curious investigators who reached down into a badger hole to grab the tail of the disappearing animal. These pioneers did not think the badger capable of turning around in its hole, but instead of the blunt end of the badger, these hapless fellows encountered the sharp end. The badger sank its teeth in with bulldog tenacity. And the story goes that the pioneer was held fast for days until he succumbed at last to the elements. I've always doubted the stories; but some people believe them. Let this be a warning to all burrow watchers to keep hands out of dens of any sort, except for wide-open, well-lighted caverns.

The badger is well equipped to make a significant hole in the ground as his burrow.

Another method of burrow watching is the stalk. Project Get Close will explain this wildlife-watching approach. Many burrows are in open places, and the residents of these dens are on the lookout for intruders. The best way to enjoy a good view of these burrows is through a careful get-close stalk and by using your binocular and camera with telephoto lens.

Sometimes burrow dwellers can be lured out into the open with food. A woodchuck in a pasture may disappear at first hint of a footstep in his domain, but he may be taught to feed openly on a rock if lured by the right kind of edible bribe. If you are unsure about their diet, consult textbooks or biologists who can shed light on the matter.

I mentioned the blind as a tool for burrow watching. Set up in the right spot, any of the blinds discussed in Project Build a Blind can be used to give a ringside seat to the burrow. Sitting in the blind until the resident of the burrow decides to put on a show can be tedious, but it's also a worthwhile wait.

Sometimes taking a stand by a burrow works well without the blind, too, depending upon the landscape. I can count on seeing a pair of burrowing owls just about any time by taking a stand at a certain cattle guard on a lonely dirt road. The guard is within 100 feet of the owl burrow. The birds always show up sooner or later. As long as I keep my distance and remain fairly motionless, the little owls will go about their business.

RECORDABLE OBSERVATIONS

The burrow watch can be a very informative wildwatch project, and you will find numerous observations worthy of recording. My prairie dog towns are a good example of what can be learned.

A prairie dog village is a complex social structure; the communication alone is very diversified. Watching closely, I soon learned that the animals lived in family groups within the society. These groups are territorial, and do not appreciate encroachment. The usual family consists of a male or two, a couple of females, and their offspring—not only young from the current litter, but also from previous litters.

The family members usually know each other by sight. I've watched "dogs" approach a burrow while a resident of the den sat high on its haunches watching. The at-home rodent would meet the incoming animal, making a close visual inspection, but also sniffing the newcomer, as well as kissing, for lack of a better term. Once you see this sign of family kinship, you will agree that animal behaviorists named it properly.

Through the spotting scope or with binoculars, I watched and recorded town activities many times, over a long period of time. I found that a male dog will stand upon its mound and bark, a sign of territorial landlordship. There is also an unmistakable bark for danger. I have been burrow watching through a telescope, eye trained on the view in the lens, when that warning bark was sounded. I always knew what it was. Overhead, a hawk or eagle might soar, or a badger might stalk the grounds. The village is one of great interaction, especially in the defense of territory. I have witnessed many disputes over land ownership, none of which seemed too serious.

These rodents fed by day; therefore, they were frequently away from their earthen lodges and quite visible, as are woodchucks and rockchucks. Prairie dogs feed mainly upon grasses, roots, seeds, and other vegetation. However, observation proved that the little rodents will eat omnivorously; if a comrade is struck down by a passing vehicle on the roadway, the carcass will serve as food.

Outside the den are the feeding adults and juveniles. The youngsters are inside, but I've often seen their heads poking out above the raised mounds that accompany just about every hole. (Some naturalists say these mounds act as dikes against flash floods.)

The intricate tunneling serves as home and protection for these rodents, but the animals are prey for many creatures—hawks and eagles from the sky, badgers, ferrets, snakes, and many other predators at ground level. Coyotes and foxes catch a dog now and then, but they cannot enter the burrow as a ferret can, and a badger may sometimes reach portions of the den and its denizens through digging.

Patterns in animal lifestyle will begin to emerge in your recordings of animal behavior and interaction. Watch the burrowing animal for a given length of time, and you will learn its ways. Watch *and record,* and you will soon be able to report repeated behavior patterns. It is this repeated behavior that allows us to draw

The entrances of burrows and dens often reveal much information. This large burrow did not hold any fresh tracks at the entrance. The many rabbit and bird bones, however, indicated that it was doubtless occupied by a predator.

conclusions about our burrowing friends, their interactions, lifestyle, and communications.

Of course, a photographic record is also advised in burrow watching. Photographing burrowing animals is often easier than trying to get pictures of roving creatures, since the burrow pinpoints the whereabouts of the animal, and repeated visits will usually result in a photo of the animal in a sedentary pose, not racing through the trees or darting through underbrush.

Nocturnal burrowers are a special problem, of course, but even these can be seen at night by using a flashlight. Point the light upward instead of directly at the bur-

rowing night-dweller. Also, wild animals seem less wary when a red covering is used over the flashlight.

CONCLUSION

Project Burrow Watch is a very rewarding wildwatch because burrows are not generally difficult to locate. To find a burrow is to find a wild animal that stays at home, or at least returns to its home frequently. Long periods of viewing and recording wildlife behavior will reward you with patterns that can often be translated into factual data.

13

Project Squirrelwatch

INTRODUCTION

The tree squirrel is found in one form or another over most of North America. From New York to California, these tree-top dwellers delight onlookers. They live in the forest; they live in the city. If you're not careful, they'll live in your house. Arizona enjoys the greatest variety of tree squirrels, but chances are, your state has its fair share of bushytails, too.

Only a remote section of northern Alaska is without tree squirrels, so the odds of squirrels living close to *your* home are highly favorable. Close? How about your own backyard? Many thousands of squirrels share their backyards with people—it really *is* that way—squirrels own the place; people just happen to live there, too.

With no travel involved, or very little, the wildwatcher can enjoy one of the most fascinating four-legged creatures on the planet. If your backyard trees don't harbor squirrels, your neighbor's might. My totally "natural" backyard has no trees, hence no tree squirrels. However, a good friend five minutes down the road has a wonderful supply of squirrels for us to enjoy. They brighten up his backyard and his life—except when they are eating all the birdseed from the feeders, chewing into the rooftop to gain access to the attic, or gnawing on a power line to short-circuit the electricity to his home.

Domestic, yet wild, that's the squirrel. He is very civilized in an uncivilized sort of way. A squirrel will learn its way around the neighborhood in no time—where the handouts and the best housing prospects are, which dogs and cats are pushovers and which to avoid, and all other aspects of life among people and their pets. He may de-

Chances are there are tree squirrels somewhere in your area, if not in your very own backyard. Squirrels have learned to adapt well to man's environment. Some people think they've learned too much about living with man.

cide to take food from your fingertips, and just when you think he's a real friend, the bushytail may bite the hand that feeds it. But even when squirrels are being pests, they are among the most interesting wild creatures living in our domain. We're lucky to have them.

OBJECT OF THE PROJECT

The object of this project is to set up a relationship with nearby squirrels and to learn enough of squirrel life so that we no longer see the little prince of the treetops as a pest, but rather as a valuable wildlife asset. Squirrels civilize well. They allow man to take part in their lives, and they insist on taking part in man's life as well. You will learn to live with and to enjoy the squirrel as you study this resourceful little animal through observation, notetaking, and learning his patterns.

EQUIPMENT

A keen sense of observation will be your most important piece of equipment. A feeder and a squirrel house will make Project Squirrelwatch enjoyable and successful. Neither is difficult to make. Also, it's wise to keep a ledger of activities on your tree squirrels, because a full understanding

The object of Project Squirrelwatch is to establish a relationship with the backyard or park squirrel. Don't be surprised to find many individual differences among these treetop dwellers.

of these clever fellows is light years away. You could uncover facts of squirrel life worthy of serious scientific attention. Binoculars are a must. Keep a set handy on your windowsill if the squirrels live in your backyard. The glass is important because we can easily misinterpret the actions of a squirrel.

One day I saw a squirrel doing a high-wire act from a power pole to a rooftop. It was carrying food in its mouth, or, perhaps, tucked under its chin, or . . . I couldn't tell for sure. But through the binocular, the squirrel carrying food turned out to be a squirrel carrying its baby while doing a "hand-over-hand" tight-wire trick on the powerline.

As with so many of our projects, squirrelwatching can be considered recreation. It is relaxing; it can be a hobby within

a hobby. A retired couple of my acquaintance began watching squirrels when they moved to a quiet little neighborhood. They now have a squirrel book underway—their own ledger of squirrel antics and activities. Careful observation, a notebook, binoculars, squirrel feeder, and house—this is the equipment that aids the wildlife watcher to take full advantage of this project.

METHODS AND PROCEDURES

Before you encourage squirrels to dwell in your backyard on a permanent basis, be certain that you won't be encouraging property damage or putting the squirrels in jeopardy. About your property—squirrels own the place—including any birdhouses and feeders they can get to, and they can get to just about anything you set up.

Whether or not you invite squirrels to live on your property or in the houses you have provided there, they may move in anyway. This house, intended for birds, became a bushytail dwelling.

Friendly and fun, yes, but before inviting squirrels to live on your property, be aware that they can cause considerable damage.

The entire area is fair ground for their inspection.

If you have a tree adjacent to your house, don't be surprised if squirrels use it as an avenue to your roof. One squirrel lover reported that his bushytail friends used a tree to gain access to his roof, and from the roof opened up a passageway to the attic — squirrels seek shelter because they know how vulnerable they are to bad weather. Cure? For the fellow with the attic problem, metal sheeting over the entry areas to his attic, coupled with a squirrel house, did the trick permanently.

Controlling the little mischief-makers is

an important part of Project Squirrel-watch. For example, use metal barriers to keep squirrels away from your pole-mounted birdhouses. These "cuffs" (inverted funnels) work; they are among the only devices that do.

One wildlife watcher thought his bird feeder was safe from backyard squirrels. After all, it was suspended on seven-strand wire between two tall poles. Certainly no squirrel could manage to climb the thin pole, grab onto the fine wire, and convey itself to the feeder. Oh, no?

Every afternoon for an entire summer that's just what one squirrel did. It

Oftentimes, squirrels take over a bird feeder. One solution is illustrated here. Even the acrobatic squirrel cannot climb out to the feeder over the 35mm plastic film containers that revolve around and around on the wire.

wrapped its legs around the highly finished pole (far too slick to climb, the wildwatcher had remarked), climbed up to the wire, and then hand over hand, as it were, made its way to the feeder, ate every sunflower seed there, and then simply jumped to the ground—free food for a little Flying Wallenda.

Squirrels have even caused power outages, major ones. Remember that their incisors continue to grow and grow; they must be ground down. That's why squirrels work away at tree bark and many other hard objects, as well as nutty foods. A metallic power line is perfect for gnawing, but, given the right set of circumstances, the result can be disastrous. The squirrel reaches the source of electrical power in the line and manages to short out the system and kill itself. One squirrel climbed inside a car engine and chewed through the spark plug wires.

About squirrel safety—don't encourage the animals to make paths that put them on a roadway. Cars kill more squirrels than all the cats in Christendom.

If you decide to invite squirrel guests to your yard, you may want to build them a home. Consider first the squirrel house. Knowledge of their natural homes is beneficial in building man-made structures. Squirrel homes include the leaf nest, loose leaf nest, and den. The leaf nest looks a lot like a bundle or ball of leaves with a hollow center; it cannot be viewed easily from below. It's really an intricately woven structure with a center lined with soft materials, such as shredded bark, moss, blades of grass, ferns, and so forth. It has a roof that is normally well made with interlaced vegetation and is quite rainproof. The leaf nest is also well anchored and appears to be impervious to wind. I watched one hold up in a wind that was clocked at fifty miles per hour. The true leaf nest is a worthy domicile for winter.

The loose leaf nest is not nearly so sturdy. Males generally build this sort of home, mostly for summertime occupancy. It's really no more than a ball of leaves, rather than a woven nest and is not very secure. Hawks have learned that if they get a good angle on a loose leaf nest, they can dive on it and capture its occupant right through the lightly constructed materials.

The true squirrel den, built in a tree hollow, is quite another matter. Lightning, insects, disease, aging, and various other

"What, me cause problems?" Sometimes the best way to enjoy and learn about squirrels is from a distance with binoculars or a terrestrial telescope.

This bird feeder is protected from Mr. Mischief by using a metal cuff, which prevents the squirrel from climbing the supporting post of the feeder.

causes create a punky juncture in a tree. The squirrel comes along and removes the pulp, making a nice hollow place, which he lines with soft materials. Several squirrels may occupy this permanent home. By gnawing with their super-sharp teeth, they keep the entryway to these dens open, even if bark tries to grow over the hole.

The squirrel house you make must offer protection. It should resemble the den in strength and function. Backyard squirrels have two major enemies—predators (mostly our own cats and dogs, along with a few neighborhood hawks that might be working the area) and the weather.

In many wooded regions, it is winter that dictates the number of squirrels more than any other aspect of nature. A hard winter will be followed by a much lower squirrel population. Therefore, a squirrel

house must serve to thwart the bushytail's enemies while offering protection from rain, snow, and wind.

The squirrel house need be no more than a wooden box with good solid walls for insulation and a hole large enough to admit the squirrels but too small for predators. If you want to build a more elaborate house, add insulation material but be certain to add it in such a way that squirrels can't rip it off, or they surely will.

A good carpenter can make a double-walled home with insulation between the walls. This offers great winter protection, but there's no guarantee that the squirrels won't find their way to the insulation material.

Squirrels are gregarious. Many may occupy a single home. Territorial disputes and male/female cohabitation among squirrels are not fully understood by naturalists. So build a large house and anchor it well in a tree, making certain it is high above the ground. Cats can reach just about any part of a tree; however, they won't be able to enter the squirrel house with its small doorway. And they will stick a nose into the hole only once to investigate squirrel life in the treetops.

This wooden structure, perhaps three feet square, must be furnished; let the residents do that. But you can help by leaving bits of cotton as well as flannel cloth strips around the squirrel house. Mattress material is very good, too.

Squirrel feeders can be open and flat, more a platform than anything else. However, a roof isn't a bad idea. It will give bushytail protection from hawks as well as provide an umbrella for him in a sprinkle. Although the squirrel hates bad weather and will seldom venture out in high winds, rain, or snow, remember that his kind remains active all winter long, so don't stop feeding when the cold months of the year arrive.

Squirrels like feeding in high places, so feeders should be placed high. Ground level is too dangerous anyway. Although a squirrel will dodge the fastest dog in town when he has a limb to jump to, put him on ground level and he's not that agile. Furthermore, squirrels seem somewhat myopic—they miss ground-level food that they find higher up. So mount the feeding platform in a tree to give the squirrel as natural a feeling as possible, with safety, so that you can enjoy his activities.

What food to feed? Local park squirrels, as well as residents of open-air zoos, are usually peanut-fed. One zoo I know of sells peanuts (in the shell, of course) to be fed to the local free-roaming squirrels on the grounds. I'm not convinced that peanuts make the best diet for squirrels, however. If squirrels feed exclusively on peanuts, they miss the important nutrients of other vegetable matter. They eat seeds of various types; they love sunflower seeds, and acorns are appreciated. (They also have no qualms about making a feast of a fallen comrade.)

Squirrels on a nearby university campus are fed walnuts. The nuts are put out in large boxes, not scattered on the ground. Squirrels jump in the box, grab a nut, and then run to bury it. Pecans are also relished by squirrels. I don't know a nut squirrels dislike, but I suppose there are some.

As always, it pays to check with biologists in your area concerning foods for wild animals. Just because a food is no good for an animal's health does not mean that the animal won't eat it. Therefore, don't feed your squirrels whatever they will consume. They may happily eat things that are detrimental to their well-being.

Houses and feeding platforms keep the squirrels around for observation. Their behavior patterns can be accurately observed through binoculars. The squirrel is a clown; his antics are interesting, but these antics are often not what they seem.

Watch especially for the breeding season. The first cycle of the year may come in early winter, another in spring. Two annual litters are not uncommon, nor is it terribly uncommon for no young to appear. When food is in short supply, young squirrels may not be brought into the world at all, which seems a rather sensible arrangement.

Mating can bring a lot of what I call "tearing around." The male comes into cycle first, so his early advances are not appreciated by the female, who often tussles with him or gives him a good nip to send him on his way. The lady squirrel is not the dominant member of the squirrel microsociety; an old boar (male) is. However, when mama squirrel has babies, watch out. She will attack not only the male squirrel, but also any intruder that gets too close to nest or young.

Another method of enjoying squirrel-watching is to take careful note of mother's training program. Squirrels are tough and rugged, but they need early training in order to make it in their world. Mother does most of the work. She teaches them how to cross power lines, for example. The shaky youngsters are often nudged out on the line, like it or not. Don't fear too much for their falling—they might fall, but a squirrel can withstand a tumble that would crush many other creatures. I saw a young squirrel topple from over twenty feet high—it thumped, rolled, got up, and dashed for its tree, where, undaunted, it directly attacked the feeder with gusto.

Watch for territorial establishment, too. Much is yet to be learned about squirrels marking off their areas. Perhaps your backyard observations will reveal facts about territory establishment. Behavioral traits are interesting—watch a squirrel use its tail. It may swish that glorious bottle-brush back and forth for balance as it walks atop a narrow fence, or it may wrap up in it as a fur coat against the cold.

See what reaction you get from a commercial squirrel call, or lacking that, hold one quarter in the palm of your hand and wrap on it rapidly with another quarter—tick! tick! tick! This sound may attract, or even anger, your squirrel neighbors.

Also watch how your squirrels thrive within the framework of the backyard ani-mal and bird community. Their individual-ity is sometimes remarkable. They may vary markedly in their reaction to other squirrels and to their environment. For example, one particular squirrel worked for over a week to reach a birdhouse until he finally made it, wreaking havoc on his feathered neighbors. Meanwhile, the other squirrels of that particular group made no attempt to follow suit, even though they had ringside seats to the bully's activities.

These methods and procedures of wild-watching squirrels are simple and basic but will help you understand the ways of these remarkable rodents. Houses and feeders, coupled with binoculars, allow long-time,

Keep records of your squirrel watching. The feeding pattern alone can be very interesting. Knowing where to build a cache of nuts can be a big problem.

close-range viewing of squirrels, but it is understanding squirrel nature that makes sense of the sightings.

RECORDABLE OBSERVATIONS

The notebook is sufficient for squirrel-watching; however, a separate squirrel ledger may be needed for serious records. What to write down? Squirrels play games—there is no better name for this activity. In my friend's squirrel yard, two bushytails frequently climb down from their sentinel posts high in a tree to raise the devil with a Brittany spaniel residing there. They know full well that even this speedy dog can't catch them as long as they remain at the base of the tree. They allow the dog to approach to within a few inches, then dart back to safety. If the dog walks away, they chatter, running back down to the lower trunk of the tree to scold until the dog gives chase again. It's great sport.

Record squirrel feats and antics. Keep a record and you will eventually have many remarkable stories to tell. Anyone who watches squirrels long enough will eventually see one spin a nut. What possible value this has in squirreldom is certainly unknown to me, but the nut-spin antic is worth watching. The nut whirls round and round the front paws of the furred juggler. Sometimes the stories are humorous only in a macabre way—take the case of the squirrels that ingeniously found a passageway to a home, where they ruined rugs, bed mattresses, and clothing.

Record behavior, as well as interactions of squirrels with each other, other animals or birds, and people. Also record the squirrel's relationship to its habitat. Out all winter, the squirrel makes certain adaptations to the weather. Record its mating season

He's thinking about what to do next. Unlike so many other animals, squirrels are seldom sedentary. In a moment, this one will be back to work on one "project" or another.

and child-rearing activities as well as its territorial imperative.

Try to identify and name your squirrels, because they can be very individual in nature. See if you can determine the "pecking order" of your squirrels—generally a large male will dominate, then smaller males, females (except when nesting, in which case the lady squirrel can become ferocious), and at the bottom of the line, the "teenagers."

And don't forget to record the sounds. Perhaps you will note variations in chattering for different events, from annoyance to anger.

See what you can make of squirrel problem-solving. Animal intelligence is not an easy area of study. Perhaps it is instinct alone that allows squirrels to solve problems; however, I've watched them unravel some real riddles.

And finally, record your interpretations of all the squirrel activities you observe.

CONCLUSION

Squirrels make interesting wildwatch subjects and are usually very close to home, in a city park if not in your own backyard. In a sense squirrels are tame; that is, they have learned to live with man. They are still wild animals, however, and are subject to the state laws that pertain to wild animals. Don't try to capture and tame squirrels without first checking the laws of your state. It may be an illegal action. And do watch out—squirrels bite. I'm nuts about squirrels but would never recommend handling them. Watch them instead. That is more revealing and rewarding.

14

Project Woodpile

INTRODUCTION

Wildwatchers often have backyard corners or larger plots of ground that would serve for wildlife if only there were cover. Without cover most living things can't survive. The woodpile should be considered a housing project, just as a bird box or squirrel den is one. Many animals and a few birds, too, will reside in a woodpile.

No cottontail rabbits lived on my property before my woodpile was on the grounds. Now there are several residing thirty yards from my back deck. I do provide some food for them, especially in winter, but shelter was the key to survival for these rabbits, not food. Before the woodpile arrived, neighborhood dogs, as well as one feline of superhunting prowess, caught many of the younger rabbits that wandered about the open grounds of my area.

Now the rabbits have a place into which to dart. I have no hard data on survival rates; I do know that before the woodpile, I saw a rabbit only now and then; now I see rabbits often. They are still in danger when they wander uphill to feed on the browse plants that grow there, but they have a haven easily reached if chased by a dog. And tabby can't quite squeeze into the narrow niches of the woodpile where the rabbits reside. But rabbits are only one species that will use a woodpile for home—there are many others.

OBJECT OF THE PROJECT

The object of this project is somewhat unidirectional—to provide cover for animals and birds that the wildwatcher wants on his property. The word *wants* is the key

A woodpile such as this one will offer a great deal of cover for a multitude of wild animals, from rabbits to pheasants.

here. Over the decades, farmers, ranchers, and homeowners have strived to repel certain wildlife from private property. My own woodpile, erected after I saw a neighborhood cat carrying baby cottontails on several occasions, immediately drew attention from an animal I did not invite to live with me—a skunk. The problem corrected itself because the skunk apparently didn't want me for a neighbor any more than I wanted him. He moved of his own volition in about two weeks; I suspect the area did not offer enough food for him. Suppose, however, that the skunk had decided to remain thirty yards from my back deck— I would have had a problem. Erect the woodpile, then take note of who moves in. Hopefully, the tenant will be welcome.

The object of this project is to use a woodpile to attract wild animals to a given area, and then, take careful note of the woodpile's residents. This is easily done by simple viewing (you will eventually see most of the residents of the woodpile, even the mice that will no doubt make homes there) and by dusting the immediate area.

Dusting has been mentioned several times before. It involves a broom-sweep of the locale, perhaps followed by a fine covering of sand sifted over the area. Anything that makes a track will reveal its presence in the cleaned area around the woodpile. The dusted area is great for plaster casts of tracks and especially useful for children who want to learn the art of casting without having to leave the backyard.

EQUIPMENT

Wood of just about any shape, condition, or type will work for a wildlife woodpile. The woodpile is a vacant apartment house. Wild animals find it and move in; they are not artificially introduced to the structure. The woodpile is "constructed" by simply dumping a pile in an appropriate corner of the property.

Since scraps are quite sufficient, cost is minimal to nothing, except for transporting the wood to the property site. You may discover wood in a junkyard or on other property during a drive around your area.

Hauling this scrap heap away may be a favor to the owner.

Consider the wood itself as a piece of equipment for this project. There are also two other wooden structures that may be used. One is a nesting box high in a tree near the woodpile. Raccoons (and the coatimundi in a few Southwestern niches) may not want to reside in the woodpile full-time, but put a nesting box in a nearby tree and it will be home, along with the woodpile.

A nesting box may also be used as a centerpiece to the woodpile. Place it at ground level in the center of the woodpile

Note here where an opening among the boards serves as a portal to the heart of this woodpile.

The brushpile of interlacing sticks can shelter wild animals. This brushpile is located in the backyard of a wildlife watcher.

with pieces of wood interlaced over it. This wooden harbor is no more than a box with one or two openings. Make the openings large enough to accommodate the animals you are interested in. If they are too small, only mice will occupy these centerboxes. The wooden box becomes a den, and the remainder of the woodpile serves as protection for this residence.

Incidentally, the woodpile need not be an eyesore. There are many ways to dress it up so you can be proud to have it on your property. Set the sticks up neatly, rather than flopping them haphazardly on the ground. Wildlife will not avoid your woodpile just because it is neat. The woodpile

may also be bordered with plants or rocks. Just be careful not to block your view of the woodpile residents with too much dressing. Also be careful about creating ambushes around the woodpile. More of that in a moment.

Binoculars, telescope, notebook, and other wildwatch incidentals round out the equipment necessary for the success of this project.

METHODS AND PROCEDURES

Before locating your wildlife woodpile, you may wish to till the soil. A tiller can be rented reasonably, and you will only need it for an hour or two. Tilling the ground breaks it up so that burrowing animals are encouraged to drill homes into the ground beneath the woodpile. A woodchuck, especially if you're in a farming area, may decide to make a home of your woodpile by building its own burrow beneath the overhead protection of the structure's "beams."

Don't make the woodpile a trap. Consider escape routes for your animals. Plants or rocks bordering a woodpile have to be strategically placed or they will serve as ambush posts for cats. If plant life is used to border the woodpile, small trees are best. These can be placed so that the wildlife watcher still has a clear view of his woodpile, and their tiny trunks are too small for predators to hide behind. Rocks

need to be small, too, and spaced so they don't make a hideout for predators.

The methods and procedures for success are ultimately simple—erect the woodpile for an advantageous view and simply enjoy following the activities of the woodpile dwellers. After a while, woodpile residents will feel safe. Then they will often allow their human neighbors to come close for good, long looks. A woodchuck family in one woodpile found that the two-legged onlookers were no threat and carried on much of their life cycle with humans only feet away.

Chipmunks, woodrats, woodchucks, mice, weasels, even quail and pheasants, will use a woodpile as a residence. When I lived in the Southwest a woodpile offered

When possible, place a woodpile/brushpile to allow for good wildlife photography.

The pheasant finds the woodpile/brushpile microhabitat adequate for survival. There is protection here from overhead attack (hawks) as well as ground attack (cats and predators). The bird is able to maneuver within the stacked wood and brush to avoid a cat.

daily shade and protection for quail. At any hint of predator invasion, the birds darted for their castle of wood. Pheasants also use woodpiles for protection, not only from predators, but from the elements as well. The center of a woodpile, while not offering the protection of a den unless you build one there, is a windbreak, and sometimes a windbreak makes the difference in survival for wintering pheasants. Also, a straw-filled center box may serve for pheasants. On a Nebraska farm belonging to a friend, we noted pheasants in a woodpile with a den, but we could never prove that pheasants actually used the den itself.

Raccoons will inhabit woodpiles, too. In fact, these interesting animals may be your best bet for woodpile homemakers. Again, remember that wild animals can raise the devil with your property; raccoons are no exception. Most wildlife watchers will agree, however, that their property can be raccoon-proofed without too much trouble. Also, raccoons that have their own houses with attending foodstuffs tend to leave your house and your food alone. Birds and animals can learn to frequent a food station, a place where food is left regularly for them. A food station can be used for any woodpile resident from quail and pheasants to woodchucks and mice. By having a food station for your raccoons, they will prowl perhaps a bit less in your garbage and garden.

The food station also allows better viewing of wildlife, especially raccoons, which will be most active at night. If you set up lights at the food station near the woodpile, the animals will soon become used to the fact that the area is illuminated and they will go about their business. They may not stay away from your porch, however, so be prepared for visitors. A camera with flash might frighten them at first, but they will even get used to that.

Raccoons semidomesticate easily. Should your woodpile be near a pond, your raccoons will probably nest on your property perpetually. A raccoon generally eats about 75 percent vegetable matter and 25 percent animal protein. In other words, it's omnivorous, and the pond will give it many plants and animals (such as frogs) to feed on.

Raccoons inhabit forty-eight of our states and Canada. They breed in winter— January, February, or March, depending on the area—and they are clowns twelve months of the year. A raccoon-proofed homesite will mean little problem from the

Brush has been interlaced on the outside of this woodpile to form a barrier. The residents of this shelter have forced an entrance hole. They take food left nearby into this shelter.

Wood bits left in an abandoned building have been carried aloft for a rat's nest.

animals and a lot of interesting wildlife-watching. The woodpile with a center den, or in conjunction with a tree den, offers a good home for raccoons. They will set up routines you can fairly well count on, too. If your raccoons begin to come to the porch a little after dark each day, you may be able to count on their regular visits for wildlife watching. But don't make pets of them. It is illegal in most areas without a special permit anyway. The raccoon might be a good pet, but it's a wild animal—enjoy it that way.

In a few areas, the opossum also makes a good woodpile resident for wildlife watch-ing. This omnivorous animal eats insects, mice, moles, birds' eggs, chicks, frogs, gar-bage, snakes, lizards, and carrion. It's noc-turnal and can be seen by using lights set up near the woodpile feeder. The opossum is not nearly as interesting as the raccoon, but he is one more prospect for woodpile wildlife watching.

RECORDABLE OBSERVATIONS

The woodpile affords the same record-able observations we generally strive for—notes on behavior, especially actions and interactions with members of the same or different species; photos; and even stories. Raccoons in your woodpile will certainly give you stories to relate and to record. One raccoon became a humanwatcher, going to one window after another every evening, sometimes sitting on the ledge for many minutes taking mental notes of the strange behavior of its two-legged neighbors. Another learned how to get a regular handout by scratching on the kitchen windowpane.

My woodpile rabbits are generally sedentary, quiet, and, if they will forgive me, somewhat boring friends to have around—until mating season. Then they can be pretty funny.

CONCLUSION

The woodpile, by offering protection, can become a homesite for many different wild animals. It serves perfectly for the wildlife watcher who has a corner of property to spare. It's cheap and easy to construct, and it brings subjects for viewing right onto your property. The woodpile also concentrates wildlife activity so that life histories of animals and some birds can be observed and recorded.

15

Project Rockpile

INTRODUCTION

Project Woodpile can be duplicated, for the most part, with a rockpile, but don't expect exactly the same residents. Wild animals are selective of habitat, including their personal domiciles, and the rockpile offers a different sort of home for creatures that prefer the geological security of stone. If you ignore rockpiles, you will pass by many interesting homesites. Project Rockpile replicates the natural stone dwellings that abound in the wild.

OBJECT OF THE PROJECT

The object of this project is two-fold; first, to study the many natural rockpiles that serve as dwelling sites for wild animals, and second, to construct a rockpile on private ground. Where I live, the cot-

tontail rabbit is a rock-dweller. His kind lives in rockpiles in many other parts of the country as well.

We also have in my locale another dweller of the rocky apartment house, rockchucks. These animals are a western counterpart of the woodchuck or groundhog. They burrow in the earthsites attending rockpiles. They're fairly interesting, although they do not have a visible social structure on the order of the prairie dog. The denizens of rockpiles, such as the rockchuck, also draw the attention of numerous predators, so taking heed of rockpiles brings sightings not only of their residents, but also of their predators.

My most exciting outdoor rockpile observation occurred many, many years ago in Arizona. I ran across a denning of serpents in a huge pile of loose rocks. The

The rockpile concept emanates from the fact that many wild animals and birds choose to make their homes in the natural rocks of the landscape. These rimrocks provide homes for deer, marmots, pika, and many other creatures.

This young marmot earns the name "rockchuck" from its natural habitat — the rockpile.

Rockpile wildlife can be monitored through the telephoto lens of the camera. Pictures become a part of the rockpile diary.

rattlesnakes were all over the rocks, and I had inadvertently slipped by several before their tails sent *no trespass* messages.

In short, I was surrounded by snakes, but it was more interesting than dangerous because I was out of reach of a strike. Slowly, I backtracked off the rockpile. The buzzing of the first snake had cued the remainder of the clan to respond in kind. The rattlesnake orchestra played a repertoire I have never forgotten. I can hear it now.

EQUIPMENT

You will need the standard wildwatch tools for Project Rockpile: binoculars, telescope, notebook, and a broom and sifter to create a dusted area for track-watching and trackcasting. The rocks themselves are also tools for this project, and, as with the woodpile, a central den can be constructed from a wooden box with an entryway for the prospective tenant.

METHODS AND PROCEDURES

You can't force wild animals to make your rockpile their abode, but you can set up the rockpile and hope prospective residents will locate it and decide to move in. As with the woodpile, don't make a trap of your rockpile; leave escape routes. You should also locate other rockpile sites to visit on a regular basis. There are generally rockpile "hotels" close to home. I have been watching a rockpile occupied by foxes for several years. The den is a burrow within the rocks, which serve to keep out intruders.

On private ground, a rockpile can be constructed with no more expense than the hauling of stones. (Be sure it's all right to take the rocks you have in mind; removal of rocks from some areas is illegal.) Place this wildlife shelter in a locale that is

A tape recorder can be placed strategically within the rockpile, especially at a denning site, for an auditory sampling of life on the premises.

Rockpiles offer nesting opportunities for birds, and also for rodents.

clearly visible for wildwatching, while not looking like a haphazard ugly heap. The rocks, most of which should be at least a foot square, may be arranged in an interesting pattern. Small trees dress the rockpile nicely, too, and their slim trunks do not create hiding places for predators.

If you build a rockpile at home, consider tilling the soil first. This loosens the earth so burrowing animals can mine it successfully. I do not have a rockpile on my property, because there are so many natural rockpiles within a few moments of my door. I have, however, helped build several.

A rockpile represents one of the better dwelling sites for various wild animals and can serve to bring onto your property animals that you may never see in the wild. For example, we built a rockpile in the Southwest; it was a rockshelter on a private property near Patagonia, Arizona, and it housed a group of coatimundi clowns. They were seldom seen by day, but a yard light aimed on their rocky home created an evening living cinema of their activities. It seemed to me that as the coati grew used to us, they came out more and more by day to feast at the feeder we had set up.

A little detective work around rockpiles reveals much about the wildlife that lives in the stone domicile. Dusting the immediate

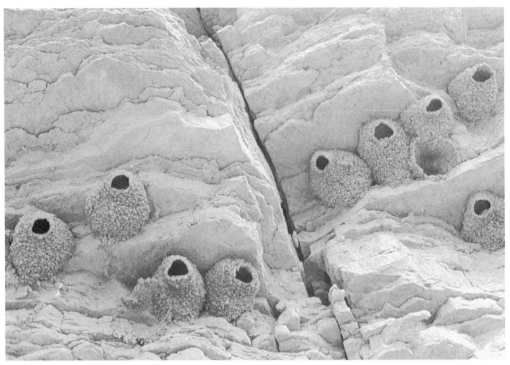

These rocks, quite close to a community, provided shelter for nesting birds.

area helps us determine who lives within; the study of droppings and bones reveals clearly the animals or birds associated with the rockpile.

Such a study also reveals what the dwellers feed on. I once located a rather strange den within a rockpile. It belonged not to a fox, coyote, rockchuck, rabbit, ground squirrel, or any other species that normally dwells in such caverns—it was the home of several great horned owls. Their tracks dominated a soft earthen shelf in front of the den, and the bones of their prey were strewn about.

The owls created a record of life around that rockpile that lured me back several times. On many evenings, I watched the big birds emerge from their rock cavern. From a few yards away, with binoculars, I had a chance to see them leaving and returning like a squadron of fighter planes. They carried back with them many animals they had caught, a few of them fairly large. One bird returned on a moonlit night with a full-grown jackrabbit in its clutches. I gained a great respect for these large, silent-flying birds as I visited their rocky lair time after time.

RECORDABLE OBSERVATIONS

The recordable observations of this project are identical to those of the woodpile project. However, be certain to make notes about the behavioral patterns that emanate from this type of residence. Animals react differently according to their homesites.

Rockpiles may also become scent posts, as this one has. The habitual use of various rocks in the region denote a specific territorial marking.

I've watched rockchucks sunning themselves in full view of eagles, hawks, and, on one occasion, a coyote. The little marmots seemed to know that they had to scurry only a few inches to reach total safety. Perhaps that is why they did not dive for the shelter at first sight of predators. The rockpile offers a secure shelter; I suspect that this security alters the behavior of its residents.

CONCLUSION

The rockpile project is very much like the woodpile project; it differs often, however, in its residents. Of course, many woodpile animals and birds also enjoy a home of rock. The opossum is one such

The high country rockpile may become a roosting or nesting site for the eagle and other predatory birds.

creature. It may live in a woodpile or tree, or within a rocky nest near your dooryard. The rockpile provides important shelter for many wildlife species, from ground squirrels and chipmunks to foxes and coyotes. Do not overlook it in its natural setting, and consider duplicating it on your home grounds. The latter prospect offers one more means of drawing wild animals close to home for study.

16

Project Waterwatch

INTRODUCTION

The backyard birdbath has been a decorative addition to many homes for many years. In fact, decoration has probably been the major impetus in erecting birdbaths. A watering station, however, is far more than a landscaping improvement. It is an attractor of wildlife that will draw many different species of bird and animal to your backyard.

The watering station has become a study platform for serious naturalists because water activities are often behaviorally important. These are activities of ritual and reason. The latter is obvious—there are reasons for coming to water; for birds, tortoises, hares, rabbits, squirrels, and other wildlife, water is one of life's necessities, along with food and shelter. But the rituals involving water are important and even more interesting to study. Watering, espe-

cially for birds, has a pattern as well as several important functions in the lifestyle of wildlife.

A watering station of any kind becomes an important part of the backyard habitat. I have built only two elaborate watering stations, both in the Southwest. The first was a shallow concrete birdbath placed at ground level in the center of the yard. Because it was in the open, it posed no threat to birds and other watering wildlife because predators could not successfully sneak up on it. Neighborhood cats tried and failed.

Bathing birds can really "get into it," and they seem oblivious at times to dangers. In my watching, however, no cat ever caught a bird at the cement dish. A hose leading from an evaporative cooler kept the dish full all summer long. Positioned above the dish, the drip, drip, drip of the

One of the author's backyard waterholes attracted desert tortoises on a rather regular basis. Although the watering site is often thought of as a birdbath only, it actually attracts many different species.

hose was in itself an attractor to birds and perhaps to other wildlife as well.

That first permanent watering station lured few four-footed creatures. It was mainly a birdbath. Our second watering station was also a cement dish; this one, however, was much larger and was placed in a far more interesting backyard, a home on the outskirts of town in the foothills of a small mountain range.

There was a large variety of wildlife roaming that region. We had many birds drink and bathe at our little cement pond, from house sparrows to roadrunners and quail. We also had somewhat irregular visits from the desert tortoise and daily visits by cottontail rabbits and jackrabbits. Now and again a fox would show up, and more than once the dusted site around the cement water station revealed the tracks of the coyote.

Much has been learned of bird behavior at the bathsite. Birds may come to drink and bathe, or just to drink, but seldom will they come to bathe only. The bath, however, is an integral and important part of a bird's lifestyle. A bath may draw more birds to the backyard than a feeder because the water is so important to them. Having quenched their thirst, the birds may enter the water, at first standing around, seemingly timid, and then dunking their heads under. They flutter their wings to spray water up over their bodies. They clean and groom their feathers with water, although it's doubtful that water plays the same preening role that anting does. (The formic acid in the ant is a much stronger and more caustic agent.)

In summer, to cool off, birds drink and dunk at the watering station. Feathers are wonderful insulation. In spite of molting, most birds remain fully feathered for flight the majority of the year. Drinking water (and sometimes holding the wings away from the body) aids in cooling them off.

OBJECT OF THE PROJECT

The object of Project Waterwatch is to meet the needs of wildlife and to observe birds and animals watering and bathing by offering some form of water in the backyard setting. On one hand, this can be as simple as filling a bowl with a hose; on the other hand, it can be as complicated as understanding the behavioral patterns of animals and birds in their most involved interactions. Water is life-giving in its quenching of thirst; it cools both animals and birds during summer heat, and it aids birds in the important function of feather grooming. Water may also be an aid during

This shallow cement backyard watering site lured the interesting roadrunner bird as a daily visitor. The dish was made very shallow to prevent the drowning of young mammals that might use it.

bird molting. So providing water for the use of our wildlife friends is a real service to them.

EQUIPMENT

Many different types of watering station work well for this project. First, there is the ordinary bowl. As basic as this type of watering vessel is, it works. The bowl can be transported easily from house to yard and yard to house, kept clean and refreshed with clear water, and if large enough will accommodate all but large bands of birds. I've had rabbits, ground squirrels, domestic pigeons, mourning doves, and many other visitors to my backyard drink from and even bathe in a large bowl. Therefore, no matter how limited the space or re-

sources, a backyard watering site can be established with an ordinary bowl.

A cement dish is also very useful for this project. It's easily made and very inexpensive. Hollow out the earth in the size and shape to accommodate the dish. A small bag of cement will build several dishes. It can be mixed right in the earthen mold with a stick and smoothed by hand. Follow mixing instructions pertaining to the specific cement. Tell your dealer what you are building and ask him about special processes that might make a better product.

The commercial birdbath is fine. It is generally beautiful and decorative; however, it can also be expensive. The pedestal type is very workable for birds but provides minimal access for other wildlife. Your yard may not offer wild mammal visita-

This simple backyard birdbath is a shallow cement structure. The rocks, which serve as perching sites for birds, are away from the edges where the birds could be attacked by neighborhood cats.

tion; I've found, however, that the ground-level watering station gives better service all around for bird as well as furred creature. Place the ground-level watering station in a cleared area so predators cannot sneak up on it.

Another piece of watering equipment is the full-scale tank, as I learned to call it in the Southwest. A tank can be made as large as necessary. It is built just like the cement watering dish but is much larger.

The binocular and notebook play a role in this project; the telescope is rarely needed. Viewing is generally at very close range, from a window. The watering station is far more than a free drinking site for visitors; in many areas it invites more wildlife visitors to the yard than a feeder. Myriad creatures interact at the waterhole, very often in unusual ways.

Birds may surprise you with many interesting behavioral patterns at the bath. If you merely glance at watering birds and animals without careful observation you will miss a great deal. So use your binoculars and notebook in this project; they are very important to its success.

METHODS AND PROCEDURES

Watching is the main method of using the backyard watering station. If the station is set up at ground level, however, dusting for tracks is also quite valuable. We found tracks of foxes and coyotes at our desert-country tank, as well as the prints of many other visitors. Deer used our backyard waterhole often in the summer, and our ground-level watering station in the Southwest also presented many close-up views of the desert tortoise. None of these encounters would have occurred with a high-standing watering device. We enjoyed watching all of these creatures.

The shallow backyard watering site is swept clean with a broom. This removes unwanted floating debris from the water. It is important to maintain the backyard waterhole, but such maintenance is very easy.

And watching was just the beginning. There was much to consider and learn.

Consider the watering station in relation to your overall backyard environment. For example, you may find that birds will not use the station as often as you thought they would. But if they don't have trees nearby to fly to after a bath, they may hesitate to dive in, because birds usually dry off and preen their feathers following a bath. This grooming habit requires a perch of some sort.

RECORDABLE OBSERVATIONS

Recording data and offering needed water to wildlife constitute the most important parts of the waterwatch. There is much to look for, much to see, and much

This is a wintering waterbox. While the backyard waterhole helps birds cool off in summer, and provides moisture for them, winter birds need a drink, too. The water dish is set on top of the box, just above the bulb, which keeps the water from freezing.

to learn and to note. Compare, for example, the activity at the bird feeder with that at the birdbath. I've watched a band of birds alight at the feeder, pushy, excited, almost shoving each other out of the way in order to dine at the "best" spot on the "best" food. That same flock of birds will then repair to the watering station with a very different attitude, which I think is the correct term.

Almost in unison, the birds will dunk, flutter, and wash. Excitement runs as high as it was at the feeder, sometimes higher, but there seems to be much less competition and "pushing." These behavioral patterns are noteworthy and very recordable.

I said that birdbaths appear to be ritualistic, and I think the "dry bath" supports this. Watch for dry-bathing at your watering site. The birds may land near the bath and go through all of the ritualistic motions of bathing without ever getting wet. I have wondered if this exhibition is a reaction to fear. Fearful of actually getting into the water, lest they be trapped there, the birds (perhaps in frustration) go through the motions of bathing even though they never get wet.

Such guesses serve as hypotheses until better data comes along. Watch for dry bathing and record it. See if you can establish a pattern. I wonder if the apparent excitement and "joy" of the birdbath are not in fact a nervous reaction to vulnerability. After all, should a predator dive in while the birds are all splashing wildly about in what seems to be total confusion at times, that predator would surely nab at least one for a meal.

Try to correlate molting patterns with bathing, too, and see if your records reveal a connection. There has been speculation that the molt triggers more frequent bathing, as well as anting. During the molt birds may also squeeze the juices from berries, applying some of these liquids to their feathers. See how these actions intertwine with routine bathing at your watering station.

Record also the actions of food dunking at the birdbath. Birds may dunk all manner of foods into their water. The boat-tailed grackle, which I observed in Arizona, often soaked bread crusts before eating them. This seemed logical enough; however, some birds also dunk seeds before eating them. This would not be for softening them, because they do not leave the seeds in the water long enough to accomplish that goal. More speculation. More hypotheses.

Watch for and record the interactions of bathing birds with one another and with other wildlife at the watering station. Birds bathing in unison are fascinating wild-watch subjects; however, birds are not the only ones who deal with a water hole in an interesting fashion.

A hare visits a backyard waterhole.

A backyard waterhole in more remote areas may attract a deer.

I watched two ground squirrels come into a watering dish once. One insisted upon drinking from exactly the same place the other was using. It would wait for its partner to dip in for a drink, and then it would nudge its partner out of the way to partake of water from the same exact spot. This shoving match went on for five minutes.

The backyard waterwatch is also very useful for recording lifelists of sighted animals and birds. Since the watering station may attract even more birds and mammals than feeding platforms do, it stands to reason that backyards with watering facilities offer many wildwatch opportunities.

Another consideration for recording is the number of times a given bird bathes in a specific time period. By recording such activity, a pattern for various species may be established. I've noted house sparrows taking four baths in a row, entering the water, emerging from their dip, drying, and then jumping right back in for another splashing free-for-all. Are consequent baths necessary for grooming or are they socially initiated? I do not know.

CONCLUSION

You can build a watering station with very little cash or time and without any special handyman knowledge. Every back-yard wildwatch post should have a watering facility. A simple, large dish of water will serve to attract wildlife, or you can build a permanent structure. You will enjoy your waterwatch while gathering many notes on the various bathing methods of different species—the vigorous bathers, such as house sparrows, and the dainty bathers, such as mourning doves. Also take note of squirrels, rabbits, raccoons, and ground squirrels as well as bird visitors at your backyard watering site.

Some birds and animals bathe alone; others make a community free-for-all of the bath house. Some bathe in a quiet and conservative fashion; others splash and dash from one end of the little pool to the other. Some bathe often; others do not.

In some areas, the maintained waterhole becomes a lifesaver for many animals and birds, especially when natural rainfall is limited. This sage grouse looks things over before coming in for a drink.

Some visitors never dive into the water at all; instead they slake their thirst and cool the physical system. Keep your notebook handy and enjoy the antics around the watering site.

17

Project Wildlife Garden and Landscape

INTRODUCTION

A garden for food and to attract wildlife; a landscape for cover and lifespace — these are the goals of this effort. Food, water, shelter, and space — they equal lifeforce. Space and territory combine as shelter, which can be provided in our own backyards with landscape and garden. Every wild animal or bird must have that ecological niche in which to thrive, and most wildlife enthusiasts have at least some space around their homes that may provide that niche.

Most homes are already landscaped, and many people already raise gardens as a pastime or vocation. By carefully structuring or restructuring the greenery around our homes, we encourage wildlife to visit our property, sometimes to stay. Most of these wild creatures do no harm. The few that do can be controlled with minor effort, such as tree cuffs for squirrels and metal coverings to thwart raccoons. Many birds are very beneficial to the garden and landscape, ridding the area of numerous harmful insects.

OBJECT OF THE PROJECT

The object of this project is to arrange the plant life around your home to attract birds and mammals of wildwatch interest and bring such wildlife in close proximity to your home, where you can watch, study, and enjoy these animals and birds. A landscape devoid of wildlife is a dull place, but you can change that by offering food and cover through plantings. Many shrubs offer food for birds as well as a place to live. A small garden may provide edibles for various wildlife friends. There are various methods of vegetative design that are

Lifespace for wildlife, that's the major reason for creating a wildlife garden. This richly foliated backyard area in the West provides lifespace for resident and visiting birds and mammals.

ornamental and decorative, while at the same time able to harbor and feed interesting visitors.

EQUIPMENT

The equipment for this stay-at-home project is very basic. You probably already have those tools normally used to maintain shrubbery and other plants around the grounds. Add to these the usual instruments of wildwatching—binoculars, a telescope if the viewing will be from long distance, and the ever-present notebook—and the list of equipment is complete.

METHODS AND PROCEDURES

Consider the landscape first because it is more complex than the garden. It is well beyond the scope of this book to describe individual landscapes for each part of the country. Those plants that thrive in the northern reaches of the continent, for example, may fail in other climates, as surely as plant life indigenous to the warmer climes would perish in a harsher area.

Decide on a basic procedure to follow for your wildlife landscape, and contact a local nursery and a conservation department officer for particulars on specific plant life to nurture specific wildlife on a

Many feeders of various types are provided, each one inviting different species to the setting.

given property. Naturally, the green-thumb artist must be careful to join only those plants that thrive together. Certain combinations of plants do not work well. The nursery expert can help you choose the right ones. Once he understands your goal, you're going to have a lot of interested help.

A basic approach to the backyard wildlife landscape is to first consider vines for the property. Vines should be selected by their value to wildlife rather than for adornment alone. That is the heart of this project — to provide backyard greenery that becomes an ecological niche for wildlife. Such vines may run along fences.

Honeysuckle — there are many types — works well. It can become very dense, offering superb cover for small animals, especially birds. Japanese honeysuckle offers excellent shelter for birds. Its thick evergreen foliage is almost catproof; cats find it very difficult to spring at any bird harbored among these vines. Furthermore, the Japanese honeysuckle has a berry that is eaten by some birds.

Creeping ivy on a shed is also useful for some birdlife and offers shade for the tinier residents of the yard.

American bittersweet vine is another backyard plant that offers food and cover to wildlife. Be certain to have both male

This wildlife garden offers shelter. The majority of the plants were selected because of their food value for birds.

and female plants if they are to serve as food for birds.

Wild grapevine will grow in certain climes and will serve various wildwatch candidates, especially some of the birds.

A backdrop of evergreen may be considered a second phase in building the backyard landscape habitat. Hemlock of various types works well. Dogwood, highbush cranberry, blueberries, chokecherry bushes — these we had in one backyard setting and they were frequented by many birds — all of these plants and many others of their class serve as a "fill" for a backyard habitat.

After vines and backdrop fillers, consider ground cover. Many plants serve here and can serve as both backdrop fillers *and* ground cover. Some of these plants are wild strawberries, sarsaparilla, dogwood,

silky dogwood, high-bush cranberry bushes, bearberry, and partridgeberry.

Trees are a fourth plant type for your wildlife landscape. The mulberry tree is one example. In a Southwest setting I had cottonwood trees nearby that housed numerous animals as well as birds. These grew along a dry riverbed, and while not directly on my property, were close enough to enjoy by simply opening the back gate.

You are fortunate if your landscape already includes mature trees, for while the addition of shrubs and vines is not totally unkind to the budget, trees can be costly — the bigger, the more expensive. Future-minded wildlife watchers who plant small trees now will reap the reward sometime later, of course.

You might also sow wildflowers on your grounds. Such flowers attract many birds

The huge tree in this backyard has been a home for many birds. Wildlife enthusiasts must protect mature trees if they want to provide homes for bird and animal visitors.

and a number of mammals. These native plants are suited to the particular microclimate of the region; therefore, they tend to grow well when properly sown and cared for. Although wildflowers seem to abound in vast meadows, they will flourish in small plots, too. They are a lot less thirsty than some of the grasses, shrubs, and flowers we often plant around our homes, but they do require some watering.

Here is how to create a wildlife meadow in miniature on the wildwatcher's grounds.

1. Choose a proper site for planting. The area must be well drenched by the sun six to eight hours each day for proper blooming. Some wildflowers do thrive in the shade, and these can be planted around the borders of the miniature wildflower garden.
2. Choose the proper seeds and plants. Best are the wildflowers that grow naturally in your region. Obviously, these plants are suited by nature to "make it" where you live, so choose your seeds accordingly. Again, the local nursery is a good source of information concerning wildflowers indigenous to your locale.
3. Plant with care. Spring or fall seeding is generally correct. Soil preparation is necessary; tilling the land six to eight inches deep promotes proper germination of the seeds. A rotary tiller can often be rented reasonably. After tilling, do not disturb the turned ground. Allow weeds to grow, then retill the soil to turn the weeds under, or up-root them by hand. Prepare the seedbed by leveling the ground surface. Mix the wildflower seeds with sand, distribute them evenly, then tamp the area to lodge the seeds in the earth. Mulch helps keep the seeds in place.
4. Manage your wildflower garden. If rainfall is lacking, some watering will be required for germination of the seeds. Mow the area in the spring of the year so seed heads will be intact as food for wintering birds.
5. Occasionally reseed. Perennial wildflowers will grow and bloom annually; it may, however, sometimes be necessary to resow a few of these plants at the beginning of the growing season.

Certain birds will be attracted to specific wildflowers. *National Wildlife* magazine notes that hummingbirds are attracted by the beautiful Indian paintbrush flower, as well as red penstemons. Naturally, all flowers that attract insects attract insect-eaters as well. Kingbirds, chickadees, downy woodpeckers, and various flycatchers will congregate around such wildflowers.

The homegrown wildflower plot will also attract butterflies, which, while not a specific subject of our projects, are always welcomed by anyone with a love for the outdoors.

There is also, of course, the garden. A wildlife garden may be of two types. It may contain the natural browse plants of the area, or it may be a vegetable garden. My neighbor reseeded part of his property with a natural grass and shrub combination, aided in the process by a county agent. While this may not be a garden in the strict sense of the term, it is a cared-for planting, and it has served to feed a number of wildlife visitors.

As everyone knows, Mr. McGregor had a terrible time keeping Peter Cottontail from his garden; vegetable gardens do bring wildlife close to home. Generally, there will be something left for the gardener at harvest time, a few carrots, parsnips, and radishes perhaps.

The wider your variety of greenery, the

wider the variety of wildlife attracted to your personal sanctuary. Each element of the habitat you add to your backyard should provide food, shelter, or both. Shelter includes a space in which to mate and rear a family.

Territorial considerations will limit the number of animals or birds that will peacefully use your wildlife landscape. But if your landscape plants provide seeds, fruits, nectar, nuts, berries, acorns, or other edibles, they will surely attract birds and many mammals as well, to feed on them, if not to live on your grounds.

Remember that the wildlife landscape works in conjunction with the rest of your "attraction center." We have already spoken of housing projects for birds and

We have a responsibility for the safety of wildlife we attract to the backyard. Birds flew into this window when visiting the wildlife garden. The attachment to the glass of a bird cutout has helped prevent the problem.

Squirrels will make a home in the wildlife landscape. Their occupancy, however, must be planned for.

some mammals. You may have a woodpile or a rockpile on your property, as well as a watering station and a feeding platform or other type of feeding structure. The plants help to complete your viable ecological niche. If your property is already replete with vegetation, you may have to augment it with wildlife-promoting greenery, as well as the aforementioned houses and feeders.

If your property is devoid of vegetation, begin planning now to make it handsome, yet conducive to wildlife rearing and livelihood. Don't forget to provide temporary as well as permanent shelter — many migratory birds, for example, need a place to stay, but only for a little while. Be certain to include these in your plans when you speak with a nurseryman or conservation officer.

Sketch a bird's eye view of your yard. Then fill in each niche with compatible plant life. Take your scheme to an expert and get help with the project, or write to the National Wildlife Federation, 1412 16th Street, NW, Washington, DC 20036. Currently, the federation is offering a "Backyard Kit" explaining how to arrange plant life for a wildlife habitat. The cost is $1.

More complete plans are available from

Where possible, the addition of a private pond adds immensely to the attractiveness of a backyard wildlife niche.

the same organization. These include several booklets on the subject of backyard plant life as wildlife habitat, landscape plans, a landscaping template and graph paper to aid in strategically locating plants, a planting wheel that describes what to plant for wildlife in each geographic region of the country, birdhouse patterns, even a personal record book. There are many step-by-step instructions in this package that will aid you in your quest for a solid ecological niche in your backyard. This kit sells for about $16. Write to the address above.

RECORDABLE OBSERVATIONS

Wildlife reacts to its environment quite specifically at times. It is not impossible to compile records of animal behavior in relationship to your landscape or garden. Specifically *how* wild creatures use the area is interesting in itself. I have many times watched territories established by birds and sometimes squirrels in a backyard niche. The rituals can be involved; so can animals' time clocks.

We were nurturing a watermelon patch in the Southwest. Now and again, a desert tortoise would pass by, eat some of the watermelon vine, nose the melon, and move on. When the next tortoise passed by, I sliced into a melon and offered it a piece. It ate with relish. Whether it came back or not, I can't say, but we always had the occasional tortoise in the patch. It was a sure lure and provided some good close-up pictures of the desert tortoise. Although the tortoise visits did not develop into recordable observations of note, they were useful in teaching us a little bit about the eating habits of these animals.

Many other animals are attracted to backyard gardens and landscapes—rabbits, raccoons, squirrels, even deer, as well as numerous birds. Watch them. They will offer many recordable behaviors. Interactions of these animals provide the most data. It's also important to take note of how the wildlife uses the environment provided by the garden or landscape.

CONCLUSION

The backyard habitat can be greatly enhanced through the development of a landscape that is planned to attract wildlife visitors and residents. The addition of wildflowers, vines, shrubs, trees, and even a garden, serves to improve a property at costs that can be quite minimal. The major goal, to bring wildlife closer to our homes, is served very well by this project.

18

Project Pondwatch

INTRODUCTION

The hub in the wheel of life for many wild animals is the pond or water hole. Myriad animals and birds return to that centermost part of their environment over and over again, not only for water, but also for food, nesting, mating, and other aspects of their life cycles.

Standing water offers many ecological advantages to any area. Such water aids in replenishing the ground-water levels and water table. It maintains the flow of streams for fishlife as well as wildlife. It creates homes for numerous animals — muskrat, mink, raccoons, beavers — and it gives food and drink to countless other animals and birds. Standing water sometimes creates drainages, and these drainages can be more replete with wildlife than the main pond or water hole that feeds them.

Water holes and ponds play significant roles everywhere. In the vast regions of Africa, watering sites spell the difference between life and death during the dry season. Water centers, ponds, and holes also play a major role in the lives of animals and birds of our own neighborhood environments where numerous interesting wildwatch subjects congregate.

I like to think of the closer-to-home watering places as ponds, those down-the-road or in-the-park pools where we can enjoy a vast array of interesting sights. Watering sites farther from home, in more pristine settings, I think of as *water holes*.

Water plants and shore plants abound at the pond or water hole. Even in a desert setting, there are green plants associated with the oasis. Such plants are vital to the continuance of many wildlife species. Ducks raise their young here, and numer-

A pond can be the hub in the wheel of life for wild animals and birds. A remote pond such as this one will attract a variety of wildlife.

ous other birds nest nearby, sometimes fed entirely by the vast numbers of insects that live about or even in the pond or water hole. Many wild animals come to drink here.

You have to look high, low, all around, and even into a pond or water hole to observe the creatures that live or visit there. Birds fly overhead and nest in trees and in the brush lining the pond; deer come to drink; interesting insects, amphibians, and reptiles thrive all around—that's the water site.

My most extensive wildwatch adventures took place along a series of ponds in southeastern Idaho. These ponds were collectively known as Sand Creek; they were built and maintained by the Idaho Fish & Game Department.

I was introduced to Sand Creek by Arnold Bowen, a man who spent a long period of his life creating new ponds and maintaining existing sites.

Sand Creek proved to be a mecca for a wildlife watcher. My notebook of sightings there would fill this book. I saw and studied moose, deer, bear, and elk at Sand Creek.

I wildwatched skunks, marmots (rockchucks), ground squirrels, bats, a multi-

The muskrat is but one resident of the pond. While ponds attract many birds, especially waterfowl, ponds also serve as homes for a number of mammals.

tude of songbirds, ducks, mudhens, herons, geese, and Sandhill cranes. There were salamanders, snakes, frogs, lizards, and toads living around and in the pond. Frequently I heard the drumming of the grouse. Mourning doves sent their plaintive cries from the trees. I saw foxes, coyotes, beavers, muskrats, rabbits, weasels, and many other creatures in my year-round visits to the pondsites.

Then I saw something I didn't expect anyone to believe I had seen. Fortunately, I was accompanied by a friend who also witnessed the same view, and even then I was hesitant to relate the incident to my family and a game biologist.

Sand Creek was locked in winter, and my eyes, and those of my friend, were binocu-

lar-locked on a group of elk moving southward, pushing through the snow. "What is that behind the elk?" I asked, even though I thought I knew. I didn't dare say what I believed the animals to be.

"Yeah, what are they?" My friend answered my question with a question of his own. I think he knew what they were, too, but when you see a wolf that far south in this modern era you shut up about it because nobody is going to believe you anyway. My wildwatch partner finally said it, and again he could speak only in questions. "They aren't . . . wolves?" he said hesitantly. But they were. Four big canines followed along the trail of the elk. They certainly were not coyotes. They certainly were not dogs. In the clear view of our binoculars the wolves marched across the ice-cream-covered field along the edge of one of the ponds. Later, I asked an Idaho biologist about the sighting.

"Impossible? No. It's not impossible to see a wolf up there," he said. "They may have come from the Island Park area, maybe even out of Yellowstone. But you did experience one of the rarest sights in this part of the country. You'll probably never see another wolf in your life out here." I never did.

Aldo Leopold, the naturalist, said that wildwatching—though he did not use that term—was an activity for the amateur as well as the professional naturalist. Leopold took his statement a step further when he suggested that we amateurs could make many very important wildlife discoveries. The pond and the water hole give us all a perfect opportunity to watch wild animals and birds, because we can repeat our visits and expand our knowledge of them. That is why Project Pondwatch is one of our more important wildwatch adventures.

OBJECT OF THE PROJECT

The object of this project is twofold— first, to locate a pond or water hole for study, then to mount a wildwatch in various ways—through slowly walking the area or by waiting in a strategic spot, either in a blind or on a stand. A treestand near a pond is often very rewarding.

We may wish to follow the nesting activity of a duck, or the interactions of various animals and birds around the water site. The goal is wildwatching, of course, and especially to learn about the denizens that dwell around or visit these natural watering stations. This project is an excellent way to introduce young wildlife watchers

to the outdoors. Because these watery areas *always* have many citizens for study, the beginner is never disappointed.

EQUIPMENT

For Project Pondwatch, the camera is especially useful because birds and some animals tend to remain longer around a pond or water hole than they do in other settings, thereby offering great photo opportunities. A magnifying glass is often welcomed at the watering site, too, especially if younger wildwatchers are along. You can use the glass to take a closer look at various plants, insects, abandoned nests, abandoned hornet or wasp castles, and many other objects of interest. Waders can come in handy, too, at the pond. Of course, they should be used in a safe manner; at the very least, tie a belt around your waist to create a seal and prevent water from entering and weighing you down if you plop into the water.

The binocular is essential at the water hole or pond, because many of the area's wildlife subjects are birds that require magnification for a better study. Furthermore, since the water site is often enjoyed through a blind or stand, you can bring animals and birds of interest "into your lap" without divulging your presence.

I do not routinely carry a telescope on my own pondwatch treks, but you may wish to set one up for distant viewing. I admit that on more than one occasion, a telescope would have been helpful, especially when I was trying to study Sandhill cranes, which, as a rule, lighted in the middle of large fields near the ponds.

Remember to take along your track-casting kit. I also suggest a daypack for the pondwatch project. Especially at distant water holes in the desert, or beaver dams

Trackcasting at the pond site is often a very successful venture. Although tracks may be slightly overemphasized because they have been set in mud, they often have excellent definition.

in the mountains, the daypack serves a pondwatcher well. It should hold provisions such as food, extra film, magnifying glass, and notebook, as well as other aids to the wildwatcher.

Finally, this project may call for a microscope, especially if young naturalists are going to enjoy the pondwatch. The microscope is used back home to study life too small to see with the unaided eye. A vial or two of pond water usually contains considerable microscopic life.

METHODS AND PROCEDURES

Finding a pond or water hole is not difficult. If you don't know of one, ask your conservation officer to help. He should know of a nearby water site for you to enjoy. If the spirit of adventure is calling, find your own water hole with a topographical map. Such maps are offered by the U.S. Forest Service, the Bureau of Land Management, and several other government agencies. Maps are also available for study at the local library. The topo map shows the more prominent water holes and ponds in a given locale and also shows waterways, which often have adjoining ponds and waterholes too small to be shown on the map.

After locating a water site, many methods and procedures are used to enjoy a pondwatch. One is to circle the area in search of wildlife homes (without disturbing nesting waterfowl or birds). Once spotted, nests in use can be observed from a distance through binoculars. You can identify abandoned nests that have no birds around them or eggs in them. These, generally, will not be used again and may be studied at will. There are many homes other than nests at a pond site. The muskrat makes an interesting abode, as does the beaver.

These two water lovers make excellent studies in themselves. The muskrat, the smaller of the two, is not an engineer, but can be interesting all the same, as they work on their houses, feed, and swim in the area.

The beaver is quite another story. He's both devil and angel, to be fair about it. Beavers can raise the devil with certain crops and can turn irrigation systems into leaking nightmares. They have been known to undermine roadways and to whittle down some very valuable trees in the orchard. They sometimes turn a trout stream into a patchwork of potholes by damming off the water and lowering the water level.

On the other side of the ledger, beavers

can do magnificent work for the watershed. Finding a stream, a pair may decide to construct on the premises. They fell many saplings and trees around the stream, using these as materials for a dam. Interlaced, these pieces of wood block out the bulk of the water and a dam is constructed, followed by a lodge. The lodge appears as a mound prepared from saplings and lengths of wood from various trees in the immediate area, all interlacing and cemented together with mud.

A beaver dam can back up considerable water, making homes for various wildlife. The pond aids in bringing up the immediate water table, which means that more plants can grow on the premises. The dam may, in a few instances, hold back thousands of gallons of water. Floods are somewhat curtailed by such dams.

As the water table rises, plant life along the banks increases further. A stretch of water that originally offered little for wildlife is now home for raccoons, mink, even birdlife from ducks to osprey. The beaver pond is a watering station for many birds and animals. One of the procedures of Project Pondwatch is to take note of beaver activity, if any, and to follow the changes in the area that the pond will surely bring.

Another pond procedure has to do with

The beaver pond offers an excellent place for wildlife study. Beavers cause water to back up in areas that would generally have little standing water at all.

You can learn about the movement of wildlife by studying the tracks at the pondsite. Tracks "take" here and are often held in the earth for a long while.

track reading and track casting. Without a doubt, the pond is ideal for these. The attending ground is generally soft enough to take and hold a track, and a multitude of stories are impressed in the land surrounding a pond. I've often witnessed the signs of birdlife stamped on the perimeter of the pond, tracks that would not have "taken" at all on harder ground.

It follows that since the pond or water hole attracts such a wide variety of wildlife, part of that wildlife will be predatory. The predators come from the sky as well as the land below. An important pondwatch feature is watching for the feeding osprey and other predatory birds in the area, as well as sign of four-footed predators that have used the pond site for hunting. Much of the life cycle of various animals and birds can be observed and recorded at a pond.

The desert water hole is often the only place you will encounter many night-dwelling creatures of the area. A number of years ago, I was privileged to enjoy a desert water hole on a property in the Tucson Mountains just outside that city. The animals had become accustomed to the lights aimed over them at the water hole; they paid no attention to them, nor to us as we sat in the comfort of easy chairs near the water. Javelina and mule deer came to the water hole frequently, and in those days another arrival at the drinking site was the diminutive white-tailed Coues deer of the region.

While that backyard water hole was ideal for wildwatching, "wilder" water holes on the desert also serve admirably for this project. Sometimes photographs can be taken of the night visitors. Flashing strobes may send your subject headlong into the night, of course, but not always. Incidentally, most of the animals I saw at nighttime desert water holes seemed to be more interested in drinking water than in making meals of each other. Certain opportunists, however, did try to capture a thirsty neighbor from time to time.

The pond site is excellent for the wildlife photographer. Many of the interesting creatures that visit or live around such a water hole offer some very interesting photo opportunities.

As always, a method of enjoying this project is note-taking as well as picture-taking. Wildlife behavior at the pond can be extremely interesting. There are numerous interactions, friendly and otherwise, as well as territorial proclamations made

The wildlife photographer can install himself at the pondsite for many interesting pictures. This killdeer was cooperative in walking by the cameraman.

around a water site because of the tremendous mix of wild animals and birds.

The procedure of taking a stand, with or without a blind, is very successful at the pond because of the activity level. This is not always true of the water hole. The more remote water hole will be used infrequently during the day by most of the desert residents. Even in the mountains, water holes often receive little attention by day from many of the mammals in the region.

The stand still serves well because of the birdlife attracted to such watersites in the daytime. You may erect a treestand by a pond or water hole. The more time you spend in that treestand, the larger your notebook will grow with important data.

Another method of enjoying the pondwatch is to build a pond on your own prop-erty, if you have the space and the water source. This is not, however, a simple project. The pond must be correctly built and correctly positioned. Remember that the water table may rise considerably around a pond; therefore, locating it near a home foundation could be very unsound. I strongly suggest contacting the U.S. Department of Agriculture or the U.S. Fish and Wildlife Service, as well as local wildlife officials, before building a pond.

Friends in Idaho had a pond built in their backyard following the Teton Dam flood in the area. That pond has attracted much wildlife; it was a good project with good results. So consider a pond on your property, but get help from the experts before construction.

Take a few samples of pond water home

Lifestyles may be studied at the pondsite. This is a muskrat house.

A pattern of visitation may be observed at a pondsite. Certain visitors, including beautiful waterbirds, may use a particular pond annually.

with you and look at these samples under a microscope. The microscopic wonderland of the pond is as rich and varied as the larger environment of the area, or even more so.

Don't forget the other wildlife that we have not treated in this project. The pond is replete with frogs, salamanders, toads, turtles, crayfish, snails, and other creatures lacking fur or feathers. Even if our interests lean to birds and mammals, there are often interactions with these little pond dwellers quite worthy of attention.

Those with underwater interest and gear, as well as water safety knowledge, may wish to use their snorkeling devices at the pond site. The underwater 35mm camera (discussed in an upcoming project) is perfectly at home beneath the surface of the water, and you can take many pictures with it at the pond and water hole. There are also glass-bottomed boats, the water-scope, and other devices that aid in seeing and photographing action beneath the surface of the water.

RECORDABLE OBSERVATIONS

The lifestyles of many mammals and birds may be studied at the water site. Mating cycles, rearing of offspring, eating habits, interactions with other dwellers of the pond or water hole—all are recordable in the usual fashion.

A study of coyotes at a pond revealed that they were destroying Canada geese

The pondsite is a place of life. Geese nesting here were aided with a "high-rise" nesting site to prevent coyotes and other ground-dwelling predators from reaching their nests.

nests as well as the young birds. The problem was cured by mounting car tires on post platforms. The geese learned to nest within the inner circle of the tire, well out of range of the coyote.

I once spent every afternoon and evening for a week at a beaver pond watching their dam-building techniques through binoculars, and a pattern was soon revealed. The same is true of muskrats and other pond citizens. Watch them long enough and you will find that the patterns to their activities are generally purposeful.

A group of ravens worked the edge of a pond I was watching. After several sessions I finally realized that the patrol was interested in nests and eggs along the watercourse. They also scavenged for carrion and refuse along the pond's edge. The arrival of the large black birds was punctual; so was their departure. Whether they found food or not, they remained along the water's edge for fifteen minutes only. That was a self-set time limit. Why? Ask the ravens. I never did figure their schedule out.

CONCLUSION

Ponds and water holes offer a concentrated view of numberless creatures. Pondwatching is very easy, and there are usually water sites within a short distance of home. This is a very inexpensive project with high returns. There are so many subjects to enjoy at a pond or water hole that it is a great place to bring the beginning wildlife watcher, who can observe, study, record, and learn about a great many wild creatures within a microcosm.

19

Project Earthmessages

INTRODUCTION

"Sign" is written upon the chalkboard of the earth by wild creatures, sometimes with temporary marks, such as tracks in the soil, and sometimes permanently, as with fossils. If you are an astute wildlife watcher, you can read these messages as clearly as a scholar reads his books. Like a detective, you will pick up each clue and mentally catalogue it until the sum total of clues unravels a mystery.

For example, you find tracks impressed in the soft earth of a dry streambed and know by their design that they belong to a jackrabbit. The rabbit was moving slowly, feeding. You find low bushes that the rabbit was nibbling at.

Then the tracks change character. Sprays of dirt reveal quick motion. From the side of the dry watercourse, another set of tracks enters the scene. These tracks be-

long to the hunting coyote. The pattern of tracks temporarily painted on the sand canvas of the dry wash narrates a story — the jackrabbit's winding course through the brush-lined streambed is a silent testimony to evasive action.

The jackrabbit is getting away from the coyote at this point. Its sharp turns are too quick for the little prairie wolf. Deep impressions in the sand indicate that the wild dog skidded off course, almost crashing into the brush along the banks of the waterbed. "That coyote went hungry if it had to depend on that rabbit for a meal," you say to yourself as you observe the messages at your feet.

But wait. Another set of tracks enters the earthen canvas. Another coyote. The rabbit has darted directly into the foliage, throwing one of the coyotes off course as it skids into the brush. Here is a tuft of

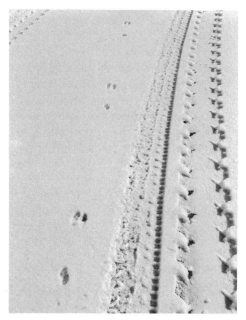

What lives here? That question is often answered by reading tracks.

an easy one to follow. A very large, hooved animal made the winding slice through the snow. There was no mistaking the print; it belonged to a moose. By employing basic principles, the moose and I eventually occupied the same little piece of territory, and he was forever captured through the lens of my camera. So you read the messages in the earth and try to answer the question, "What happened?" which leads to, "What lives here, and can I find it for wildwatching?"

Around ponds, streams, lakes—anywhere the land has been softened by moisture, that chalkboard in the earth appears. Along the ocean, but also where streams once ran or where water courses now and again, sign is impressed to be left for your observation. Wherever there is bare ground, the imprints of animals will "take."

coyote fur grabbed by a thorny bush as a memento of the chase. Now the other wild dog closes in. And the climax of this story is told by scattered rabbit fur. Only two sets of tracks leave the scene; both of them are canine.

The astute nature lover finds such wildlife tales every time he experiences the outdoors. They are everywhere. Sometimes we study these signs to learn what happened. While we were someplace else, an event took place, and we want to know about it. We find out from the clues captured by the landscape. But there is another reason for studying the marks left by wildlife.

Sign helps us find wildlife. It answers the question, "What lives here?" You search the area for what you know lives there or you stay on a trail until you catch up with the subject of your interest.

I was on such a trail in winter. This was

The soft earth near a streamsite is a good "chalkboard" for the track. This bear track was located in the high mountains.

But sign is much more than tracks. The environment also captures feathers and bits of fur on branches, tree trunks, fencelines, even rocks and woodpiles. There are droppings that not only indicate the presence of a given animal, but tell also of its lifestyle.

You should train yourself to read and to interpret each sign, whether it is impressed in the earth, trapped by foliage, marked in snow, or caught by a bush. We learn by the messages in the earth, and we use them to find our subjects. While this project may at first seem to be more suited to a Natty Bumpo of the backwoods than a modern wildlife watcher, the truth is, it's an everyday pleasure that can take place a stone's throw from your home.

You need not go far to find the messages left by wild creatures—a snake's winding imprint left at the edge of a pond; a trail through the snow; the leavings of the predator, from tiny chipmunks to large marmots; tracks held fast by dried earth; transitory marks in the sand that will be wiped away by the wind.

OBJECT OF THE PROJECT

The objects of this project are numerous. Two obvious reasons for studying the signs left by wildlife are to find candidates for the wildwatch and to decipher what events took place. Tracks and other signs can lead us quietly to first-row seats in a wildlife drama. They help us locate and watch wildlife subjects that do not even know we are near and take excellent photographs of these subjects and events.

Another object is to make a collection of cast tracks for study. Some wildlife watchers also build a lifelist of tracks they have encountered. These may be kept in note-

book form or in a photo file with attending data sheet.

Nocturnal animals are known to many wildlife watchers mainly through their tracks and sign; therefore, another object of this project is to learn something of night-dwelling creatures that we may never see in nature.

We learn tracking, even over broken ground, by taking note of disturbed vegetation that indicates passage or feeding of wild animals. Even distorted tracks in broken earth can be read by the practiced wildlife watcher.

EQUIPMENT

For Project Earthmessages, you will need an old broom, toothbrush, a sifter, some plaster of Paris, a water canteen, a roll of narrow stiff paper, a tin can, plastic food bags, a small tape measure, and a camera with close-focus lens (optional). Also optional is a can of talcum powder with which to dust tracks for better picture-taking contrast.

A notebook or notepad for sketching tracks and/or other signs is useful. The notebook or a photo album may also be used to include data about the sign, such as the story it reveals. A field guide is also very valuable, if not entirely necessary to the success of the project. *A Field Guide to Animal Tracks* by Olaus J. Murie and *Field Guide to Tracking Animals in Snow* by Louise R. Forrest are good ones. Quiet footgear and clothing, soft but protective, are also helpful when following a track.

The broom is used to dust clear any area where the wildlife watcher wants to capture a track. Feeders and watering holes are excellent sites for dusting. A sifter, which is a wooden frame covered with

The sifter aids in preparing the ground to take a track. The earth is cleared of old sign by covering the specific area with new, freshly sifted earth.

screen, applies a covering of fine sand over the dusted area to ensure good tracks. Plaster of Paris is the molding medium for casting a track. The water canteen holds the liquid for the plaster, and the tin can contains the mixing material. A strip of stiff paper is used to surround the track, forming a dam to hold the plaster. Use the toothbrush for cleaning the cast.

Plastic bags hold scats for further study. Measure the length and width of each interesting track with the tape and record track pictures with a camera with close-focus lens. The field guide serves as infor-

mation center concerning the individual track and the animal that made it.

METHODS AND PROCEDURES

Tracking and trailing give you excellent exercise; quiet relaxation in the outdoors; an opportunity to locate, enjoy, and learn about wildlife; and a chance to study animal behavior. Snowtracking offers some of the greatest rewards. However, snowtracking is much more than finding fresh sign and walking directly in the path of that sign. Snowtracking means looking for mammals, wary animals that seem to sense that tracking them in snow is easy. These creatures, whether deer, elk, moose, or mountain lions, know how to survey their backtrails.

When we take a tracking trail and remain directly on it, we soon give away our position. The animal or animals of interest break out and put distance between themselves and us, and we never see them. In snowtracking, do not remain directly on the trail; move off to the side of it. Study the terrain ahead, and use the lay of the land to best advantage. Guess at the animal's route, and try to interpret where it may be going, where the tracks are leading to, and see if you can cut him off. If you can't get up ahead, and you must remain directly on the trail, don't move all the time. Walk and freeze; walk and freeze.

I was following a moose trail not long ago. It was clear, and I knew it had to be fresh because it had snowed only six hours earlier. Initially, I walked directly along the path made by the giant deer. In a short while, however, as soon as I suspected that I was getting close to the animal, I left the trail, climbed the side of the canyon, and looked ahead with binoculars to see if I could spot the moose. I could not.

So I took to the trail again, but again left it when I had gone a few hundred yards, this time swinging in a circle well ahead in the direction the animal was taking. My U-turn maneuver paid off. I had walked ahead of the animal and had cut him off. The wind was in my favor, and I had a ringside seat to the mountain moose as he walked slowly along. By stalking, I ended up with a fairly decent photograph of my moose. Had I continued to follow the animal, I'm sure he would have discovered me and made a dash up-canyon, leaving me well behind.

Even animals not noted as sharp-sighted see movement quite well. Conversely, I've remained motionless and not entirely hidden in the path of keen-eyed antelope, only to have a herd walk within a few yards of me.

I've seen trackers ignoring the direction of the wind as they pace along. If the wind is directly at the back of the tracker, the animal up ahead is going to detect the wildwatcher's presence. But you must travel in the direction of the trail, right? Right, but use the oblique methods spoken of above as much as possible when the wind is wrong.

Quiet is advised, too, hence the suggestion for soft clothing and boots or walking shoes that allow a quiet pace. The animal of interest is not only watching its backtrail, but also listening for the approach of any other creature.

The same tactics are used to trail an animal when there is no snow on the ground, and though this is a difficult feat, it's not impossible, especially if there happens to be damp earth, or "washes" (western waterways of soft sand, usually dry), trails along waterways, or other conditions amenable to taking and holding a track.

In tracking, remember that trailing the animal is only half the reason you're on his path. Tracking and sign reading help us understand animal behavior and motives. We can determine whether the animal was running or walking, and if it encountered other animals. What reaction did the animal have to such an encounter? Was the animal hunting or feeding? Fighting? How many were there? Which were males or females and what clues did each give you? Where were the tracks leading to?

This last one is important, not only for finding wildlife to watch, but also for learning about the animal's behavior. A band of deer were feeding in cultivated fields by night but leaving the fields before dawn. By trailing the deer, I discovered a pattern of behavior—feeding at night, walking from the field to a small water hole, and from the water hole to a bedding area in a canyon. During the day, the animals rose from their beds from time to time, feeding on browse plants. Then, at dusk, they meandered once more toward the farmer's fields.

Trailing helps us discover bedding grounds, dens, and other home sites for many mammals. I've enjoyed following the trail of a sidewinder rattlesnake in the Yuma, Arizona, desert. The strange path left by the snake rewarded me with a story of his actions, culminating with a sighting of the snake itself.

In the scat of a mountain lion, much evidence of deer hair presented itself; the scat of the little gray fox showed the same. I reasoned that, since no fox is going to down a deer of any size, the fox must have happened upon the mountain lion kill, in spite of it being covered over with dirt and debris, and helped itself to a meal.

Wild turkey droppings reveal the sex of the birds. The male generally leaves a J-shaped deposit. The female's is some-

The owl pellet is another form of sign. Here, an owl pellet is shown with an owl feather. The pellet contained whole bones of the cottontail rabbit.

what amorphous, generally round, but not with a definite global shape. The owl pellet reveals, too, what the birds are feeding on. I located two owl nests on a remote abandoned homestead. The area looked perfect for mice, and I'm sure the owls did feed on mice; their pellets, however, showed almost exclusive cottontail rabbit predation at that particular time.

Look also for signs of feeding. In the Southwest, the study of javelina, the peccary, often starts by locating their "restaurant." Javelina are not dainty eaters. They chew big bites from prickly pear cacti, their favorite fare, and they nip the green blades of Spanish daggers and other similar plants. They also excavate wild onions, sometimes leaving considerable cavities in the soil.

To ignore such sign is to pass up a great deal of information concerning javelina, as well as their whereabouts. So tracks alone do not constitute sign. For example, birds of the gallinaceous group, such as quail, leave many diggings and scratchings in the soil. Squirrels may leave caches of food.

At your signpost or any feeding site, you can dust the area with a broom to take and hold a track. If you wish to prepare an even better surface for track-holding, use a screen—a fine wire mesh tacked over a pinewood frame. A few handfuls of dirt sifted through the screen directly on top of the dusted area will prepare the ground to reveal the track of even a mouse. If you have your water canteen along, sprinkle the dusted area lightly for a longer-lasting track.

RECORDABLE OBSERVATIONS

The wildwatcher may wish to photograph his track finding. I find that track photos can be made very successfully with a 35mm camera fitted with a 35mm (semi-wide-angle) lens. Such a lens allows close focusing with very little distortion.

Black and white film is entirely sufficient for this project—try Kodak TMAX 400 ASA. A tip—test the camera angle of the track. Even the slightest change in light can improve a track photo many times over. I learned this lesson from tracking. You will find that if you move your head from side to side, altering your perspective, you may see a track, quite literally, in a different light. I've seen depressions in the earth that did not reveal themselves as tracks until I changed position and viewed them from a new angle.

Finally, try a light dousing of talcum powder in the track if it does not stand out. The talcum may improve the contrast between the track and the earth in which the track is impressed. A flash may be needed to photograph a track in dim lighting.

Use the notebook or photo album for recording track data; use a field guide if you are in doubt as to the range of data to record. The Murie guidebook speaks briefly of each animal, especially concerning its nature. With this knowledge, the wildlife watcher knows what to look for in a track. For example, Murie shows the raccoon's track, as well as mentioning the ways of the animal briefly and describing its scat. Claw marks on trees, cavity dwellings, ground dens, and other features aid in identifying the raccoon's earthsigns. Remember that all recordable track data may be kept in a lifelist as well as a notebook or photo album.

Measure the tracks carefully for your records, not only the length and width of forepaws and backpaws, or of birds' feet, but also the distances *between* the tracks. Such distances can aid in revealing the size of the wildwatch subject as well as its motion. Murie shows a distance of two and one-half inches between the tracks of the tiny jumping mouse, for example, indicating that the little animal was hopping along, not walking along.

Tracks may also be preserved. Having come upon a nice, deep track, hopefully in earth that was soft enough to take a sharp imprint, encompass the track by pressing a stiff cardboard frame around it. Such frames can be made from construction paper or other stiff paper bought from a school or office supply shop. The "corral"

of paper creates a dam to contain the plaster of Paris.

Remove the plaster from its container, and transfer it to the tin can. Add water to the plaster. Stir rapidly with a stick, making a thin mixture. When this mixture is right, it resembles thin pancake batter. A thin mixture makes for a better cast because it fills each feature of the track, whereas a thick paste fails to follow the exact outline of the inset in the ground.

Fill the track carefully, without splashing the plaster. Hold the mixture close to the track as you pour. If you ladle it in

Plaster of Paris carried in a plastic bag, a water canteen, and a container and knife for mixing make a good trackcasting kit.

The mixture is made thin enough to fill the track well.

The liquid plaster of Paris is poured directly into the track. This track is so deep that a dam is not needed.

A trowel is used to lift the set plaster track from the damp earth. An old knife can serve the same purpose.

from on high, the force of the falling plaster may break down the walls of the track, distorting its true shape. Now wait. There is no prescribed time limit, because atmospheric conditions have much to do with drying times. However, an hour is about average. If you leave the immediate area while the plaster dries in the track, be sure to mark the track site, perhaps with a blaze orange ribbon, so you can find it again.

After the plaster looks dry, pick up the paper dam along with the plaster cast of the track. If the plaster is hanging onto the ground, you may have to carefully pry it away by digging well beneath it with a sharp stick or a knife.

At home, wash the plaster cast with water and a soft-bristle toothbrush to remove any clinging dirt. You will have a "negative" of the track, as it were. To make a positive, the cast will have to be impressed into another medium. It can, of course, stand on its own, a casting of the depression in the soil; however, this is not an accurate representation of the track itself. A stiffer plaster of Paris can be used to hold an impression of the track or tracks if you choose.

Finally, don't be afraid to try other plasters. Plaster of Paris has been a standby for years, and it was the only medium I used until recently. I found that drywall joint

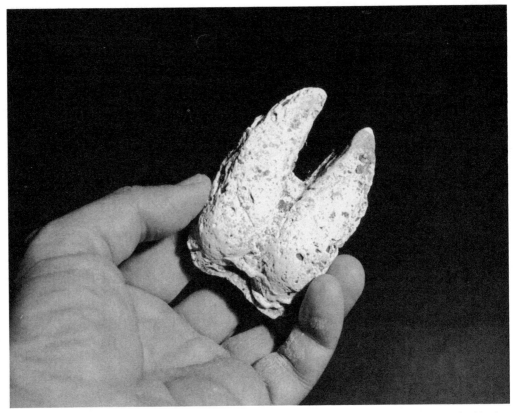

The plaster cast of the track is essentially a negative and not a positive. In order to make a positive track of it, the plaster track can be pressed into clay.

compound works well for cast impressions of tracks.

CONCLUSION

Reading earthmessages is an important part of wildlife watching, both to tell the story of animal behavior and to determine the wildlife species that live in a given region. The project also has value as a relaxing hobby in its own right, especially if tracks are cast in plaster, a photo album with data sheets built, careful notebook entries made, or a lifelist compiled.

Don't leave nonmammals out of the picture. Reptiles leave earthmessages, too, as do birds, especially ravens, pheasants, quail, dove at the water hole, wild turkeys, Great blue herons, Sandhill cranes, geese, ducks and many others. Don't forget bones, feathers, fur, scats, and pellets. They, too, reveal stories of wildlife behavior.

20

Project Shutterbug

INTRODUCTION

The U.S. Fish and Wildlife Service reported in 1970 that America had five million wildlife photographers. Only five years later, that agency had to alter the figures. A minirevolution had taken place among outdoor picture-takers. America now had *fifteen* million wildlife photographers. The ranks of the outdoor shutterbug have grown steadily ever since as wildlife photography has been added to the list of exciting subjects for shutterbugs.

The camera is so much a part of our own wildwatch projects that oftentimes I have had to remind myself to include it under Equipment. The wildlife photograph is a lifetime record of an event, the sighting of an animal or bird. The pictures can be collected in a notebook by themselves, or they can illustrate data that appears in the wildwatcher's notebook.

While the photograph supports many of the projects in this book, the reverse is equally true — many projects in this book support the photograph. The photograph augments the trackwatching project, for example, and our upcoming "Project Get Close" supports wildlife photography.

This approach to becoming an outdoor shutterbug is basic. This is not a guide for the professional film-taker; however, this project does present workable methods garnered from years of practice photographing the outdoors.

For those who wish to become experts with the outdoor camera, I suggest a great deal of practice. My brother, who is a professional photographer, often says that the difference between a pro and an amateur is the number of frames used — the pro shoots a lot more film than the amateur.

Further reading on the subject is also

recommended. Libraries and bookstores are filled with titles on outdoor and wildlife photography. There *is* a difference between the two, by the way. One can take a lot of outdoor photos without ever shooting a single frame of a wild animal. A book I recommend for both outdoor and wildlife photography is Kenn Oberrecht's *The Outdoor Photographer's Handbook,* Winchester Press, 1979.

OBJECT OF THE PROJECT

The object of this project can be stated quite succinctly—to enter the field of nature photography and to take good photographs from the start.

EQUIPMENT

A worker is no better than his tools. That phrase has been around longer than the Mendenhall Glacier, but it's as true today as it was when it was coined. The wildlife photographer may be able to locate his subjects, get right next to them, use available light to best advantage, and for all intents and purposes have the animal or bird almost pose for him, but if the camera is wrong, chances for a great photograph are slim to none.

Most beginning wildlife photographers follow a similar path in choosing equipment. They are not certain of their tenure in wildlife picture-taking, so they hope to get by with marginal equipment. This, in the long run, is an expensive way to go. Buying wrong camera equipment means rebuying correct equipment later on.

The camera is an investment. It will record family history, produce vacation slide shows, build pictorial memories of your friends and neighbors, even illustrate files of your possessions for insurance pur-

poses. So don't shortchange yourself with either inferior or incorrect photo equipment. You are going to *like* wildlife photography.

Good cameras are no longer financially out of reach. There are many superior models at modest cost, and used cameras are very often a bargain. Check the classified ads in your local newspaper for top-brand used cameras. A camera is generally good for many thousands of shots, and the average camera is still like new five years after purchase.

Perhaps things will change, but for the moment there is only one supreme wildlife camera—the 35mm format. I hold the medium-format camera (120-film size) in high esteem for landscape pictures and studio work but can find no earthly reason to burden myself with one on the trail of wildlife pictures.

Furthermore, I can't always find the exact 120 film I want, but every drugstore from Portland, Maine, to Portland, Oregon, has 35mm film. The 35mm camera is relatively economical to purchase, even new; it will last for decades; and it shoots film that is far less costly than the medium- or large-format camera.

You should purchase your 35mm camera in the single-lens reflex style. Period. Rangefinder cameras are excellent for certain work. The shutter release of the rangefinder camera is generally very quiet—no mirror noise. Rangefinder cameras may also be quite compact; however, the single-lens reflex camera allows the photographer to view right through the "taking" lens. Essentially, what you see through the eyepiece of the camera is what the lens "sees." You can't possibly have a problem with close-up work, or with long-range photography.

Furthermore, you should insist that

your 35mm single-lens reflex wildlife camera have a built-in, behind-the-lens light meter and that the camera operate automatically as far as exposure is concerned. On my particular cameras, I set the shutter speed to "A" for automatic. Then I select the lens opening (aperture) for the F-setting I want. Now I need only focus and shoot. The camera does the rest.

You don't want to have to try to "read" the light out there with a light meter, then adjust your aperture and/or shutter speed. Instead, the shutter speed and aperture setting are, in essence, preselected. For example, on a bright day where I live, my camera's shutter speed is set to "A" for automatic. With 400 ASA film speed, I can set the lens for an F-11 aperture. The shutter speed will automatically select somewhere between 1/250th of a second to 1/1,000th of a second, depending on filter and shadow.

With these settings, my wildlife pictures are free of "camera shake"; they will have good depth of field; and they will "stop" most action—all without my altering the lens opening or shutter speed any further after making my initial settings.

When you aim at your subject, the light in the center of the lens dictates how the camera will be set. The aperture and shutter speed are preset now, and all you have to do is focus and snap the picture. Various cameras use different methods of automation, of course, but the end result is the same—the autometering system takes the worry out of setting the correct camera exposure.

The camera must also be capable of accepting interchangeable lenses. Although our goal is wildlife photography, which is accomplished usually with a long or telephoto lens, there are also going to be many close-range photo opportunities in the

The single-lens reflex 35mm camera is the choice of most of today's wildlife photographers. It allows through-the-lens viewing of the subject, as well as proper metering for light.

field. For example, you may wish to photograph a track in the soft earth along a pond site. It may be possible, and at times even desirable, to step back and focus on the track from several feet away with a long lens. But this method will not prove practical all, or even most, of the time. Instead, you stop and pop the long lens off to install a shorter focal-length lens. Then get close to the track, framing it perfectly, and capture it on film.

When shopping for a new camera, consider buying the body first. This is a very common approach to camera purchasing. When you have the correct 35mm camera body, look for those special wildlife lenses. I believe that you can accomplish all your general field photography with a doubler and two lenses, the 35mm lens and the 300mm lens. The "normal" lens for a 35mm camera has a focal length of about 50mm to 55mm. This means that with a 50mm lens in place, the image will appear one-to-one. It will be neither magnified nor reduced at the film plane. That's very

The basic outfit includes the 35mm body; a semi-wide-angle lens (shown on the camera); a telephoto lens, in this case a 300mm; and a telextender or doubler, this one 2X, or two power.

nice; however, a normal lens gives you neither of the desired effects you normally need for close-up or long-range work. The 35mm unit is really a semiwide-angle lens. It is, I believe, perfect because it allows very close focusing, and a wide-angle picture, both without undue distortion of the subject.

The popular 28mm wide-angle lens for the 35mm camera does take in a greater piece of the landscape, but it also has more distortion than the 35mm lens. Go higher than 35mm, and the wide-angle, close-focus aspects of the lens diminish. I cannot recommend the 35mm lens strongly enough. It will not, however, serve for the hawk perched on a limb 100 feet away. For this, you need a longer focal-length lens.

I have selected the 300mm lens as my standby for several reasons. As lens length grows, one very good thing happens—the image increases in magnification. A 100mm lens is about 2X—two-power. A 200mm lens for the 35mm camera offers about 4X—four-power. A 300mm lens renders about 6X—six-power—magnification.

Even the latter power is, admittedly, not very much magnification. However, as focal length increases, the big lens gobbles up more light. Long lenses with a lot of light-gathering power cost a lot of money. Furthermore, the long lens not only magnifies the view, it also optically magnifies camera shake. Even the most steady photographer will find it difficult to hand-hold a very long lens, not only because of magnification, but also due to sheer size and weight of the longer telephoto unit. And if you open the aperture of the lens to allow for a faster shutter speed, you lose depth of field.

I like the 300mm lens. Therefore, my 35mm "outdoor" camera has but two lenses, a 35mm semiwide-angle for general picture-taking and a 300mm telephoto lens for most of the actual wildlife shots. I am not a fan of the "mirror" telephoto lens. The particular ones I tried did not render as sharp a picture as my straight telephoto lens.

I do, however, have a telephoto lens enhancer. This is a doubler or teleconverter. It is in itself a lens that attaches to the camera body to which my 300mm lens attaches. In my system, which is a Nikon, I have a TC 300 auto-indexing teleconverter lens that turns my 300mm lens into a 600mm lens. Now I have 12X magnification instead of 6X magnification — but not without a price. The Nikon doubler happens to be a supremely good one; it does not destroy the clarity of the picture at all. When attached, however, that 300mm lens now gathers less light and is much harder to hand-hold. Therefore, I use the doubler only when I can employ a window mount or tripod to hold my camera steady.

Zoom lenses are good; however, I would want a zoom to range from 35mm to 300mm with excellent quality, and that is asking for a lot. So my basic 35mm wildlife system includes the body as described above, a 35mm lens and a 300mm lens, along with a 2X teleconverter to multiply the "power" of my 300mm lens into a 600mm lens. I feel that with this setup I can handle the usual wildlife photo options available to me where I wildwatch.

Filters are necessary for wildlife photography. There are numerous filter types on the market; each one has its specific purpose. I have boiled my own 35mm filters down to only three. For color film, I use a Skylight filter. This filter protects the precious lens from smudges and modest bumps, and it absorbs the ultraviolet rays and tends to "cut haze."

For black and white photography, which you may or may not want to get into, a yellow filter makes sense because it, too, protects the lens. It absorbs excess blue and darkens the sky, as well as accentuating clouds for those general scenics you may wish to snap.

My third filter can be used for both color and black and white film. It is a polarizer. The polarizer darkens the color of a blue sky and also reduces glare. I find the polarizer excellent for photography at the pond or stream edge (even below the water level), and for photographing animal or bird tracks. Remember that with your through-the-lens viewing, the effect of the polarizer is seen as you turn its adjustment ring. Furthermore, because you have behind-the-lens metering and camera automation, you do not have to adjust the exposure of the camera for each filter you place before the lens. What light each filter cuts is compensated for automatically.

You may wish to add a strobe or flash to your wildwatcher's camera kit. In some dim recess of the woods, a good photo may present itself and the flash will shed light on that subject. Seldom, however, will a flash of any sort work for actual animal or bird picture-taking because the subject is usually too far away for the light to reach it.

What about a motor drive? There are true motor drives that, when used in the auto mode, race the film through the camera at several frames per second, and there are auto-winders, which also advance the film automatically, but at a slower rate. You don't need either one, but a true motor drive will allow for some very interesting action shots that you may not get otherwise.

I made a good sneak on a flock of sage hens in a grassy depression one day. When I got close, I placed the camera to my eye and tried to focus as I paced forward. Of course, the birds put up with only so much of my advance. Whir! Up they flew. My motor drive, however, went into operation and "stopped" a few of these big grouse in midair. Without the motor drive, I *may* have gotten a good photo, but probably not. If you wish to stop a deer in stride or a bird in the sky, the motor drive may be your ticket. Decide on a motor drive before

This picture resulted from the use of a motor drive. Without the drive, the shot probably would have been missed. Many excellent action shots can be achieved through good timing and a fast shutter speed, without the motor drive unit.

buying your 35mm camera. Then you can purchase the proper camera for the drive and the proper drive for the camera.

Camera bugs can buy more gadgets and gimmicks than model airplane enthusiasts ever thought of. I have tried to keep my wildlife and outdoor camera gear to a minimum. There are a few additional items, however, that are necessary to successful picture-taking. The tripod is one. Especially when using a long lens, the tripod can spell the difference between a blurred photo and a sharp one. The window mount generally used to support a telescope works with a camera, too, and I have often employed this steadying device, especially when the doubler makes my 300mm lens into a 600mm lens. I also have a hard camera bag. This protects the camera, lenses, and accessories.

I use several types of film for wildlife photography. My workhorse is Kodachrome 64. Resulting 35mm slides render a wonderful sharp image, creating beautiful slide shows. Even at fifty inches width on the screen, the picture remains clear and realistic with Kodachrome 64 and will remain so years later.

There are times when an ASA (film speed) of 64 is too slow for my needs. Then I switch to Kodachrome 200, a faster film. I do not like the color rendition of Ectachrome as well as Kodachrome. I have also detected eventual fading in the former. Without a faster color film, there are times I would have no picture at all. Many wildlife photographers will prefer a color print film over the above choices. This film results in "pictures," rather than transparencies.

I enjoy black and white photography. Many wildlife subjects, while prettier in color, are just as appealing and serve the wildwatcher's purposes as well or better

This picture was taken with the use of a Bushnell window mount, used to steady the camera when the photographer is driving backcountry lanes in search of good pictures.

in a black and white photograph. Several black and white frames cost less than a couple color shots, too.

I enjoy developing my own black and white film and printing my own pictures. Many local community colleges offer darkroom courses. They are fun and the basics of the subject are easily learned. These courses will not instantly turn the beginner into Ansel Adams, but the basic darkroom course will teach sound photography procedures. You will be able to snap a decent black and white shot, develop your own film, and produce a clean, crisp print in a few weeks.

My only black and white film for 35mm outdoor photography is Kodak's TMAX 400. This is a fast film, allowing a quick shutter speed with relatively small lens aperture for good depth of field. The result is a sharp negative, developed at the local camera shop or by you, yourself. On a bright summer day, I shoot at shutter speeds of 250th of a second to 1/1,000th of a second with an F8 to F16 aperture when using TMAX 400, and that includes a yellow filter in front of the "taking" lens. Developed in TMAX developer, this film produces a sharp negative that will make hundreds of prints if called upon to do so.

METHODS AND PROCEDURES

By using your sharpened senses, you not only see and hear better in the outdoors, you also see "wiser." Tuned senses aid

This nesting golden eagle was captured on black and white film using Kodak TMAX 400. The distance of the picture was great, and the negative had to be enlarged many times. Black and white nature photography offers a good record at a comparatively low cost to the wildlife watcher.

greatly in getting those wildlife pictures that are more than mere snapshots. Your knowledge of calling or luring wildlife subjects aids in photography, as do your stalking techniques. Here are some methods for wildlife photography that serve as a shortcut to better pictures.

Light is important to the photograph. In the studio, we set up umbrellas, strobes, backgrounds, floods, and many other devices to artificially create the right kind of light in the correct intensity, emanating from the most beneficial direction. Outdoors, our control of light is more limited. The way we use light, however, even in the wildworld, will dictate how sharp our pictures are going to be. Sometimes a strobe can be used to direct more light on the

subject. I do not enjoy packing any more photo equipment than I have to, so strobes seldom find their way into my outdoor photo kit. A mirror can be used to bend light toward a subject of interest, but this trick works only when the animal or bird is sufficiently sedentary to allow us to flash sunlight at it.

Try to maintain a field position that has the best picture-taking light. If walking a field, elect to walk with the sun at your back instead of in your face. Naturally, it's pretty difficult to maintain this position, since what goes away from camp must return to camp. But if you're starting out in the afternoon, put the sun to your back, wind direction permitting. When you return to your point of origin, the sun will be fading anyway. If you choose a place for a blind or stand, position yourself with the sun in your favor. Be wise about light. Attempt to maneuver so that the best light is on the subject, not in your lens and on your face.

Sometimes waiting for a split second before tripping the camera shutter will alter the light situation in your favor. I was trying to get a photo of a cottontail rabbit, a rather simple task as wildlife pictures go. I noticed as I focused the lens that the dark eye of the rabbit was lackluster in the viewfinder. By waiting a few moments, the rabbit turned, and instead of the dull eye, there was a glint. The resulting picture was much better. Reflection in the eye of an animal or bird gives the picture a moving quality that says "life."

Try the backyard for your first wildlife pictures. Backyard birds and squirrels are more familiar with humans than their wild cousins, and they may stick around long enough for some very interesting "poses." It's no trick to set a camera up on a tripod near the bird feeder or squirrel house,

Calling wildlife can aid the photographer in getting a frame-filling picture like this one.

using a long cable release for your shutter. This remote-control photography will allow some remarkable pictures, since the subjects never see you.

A cable release is also workable at the den or burrow. You can remain in the background until your subject poses for the best shot. One wildwatch enthusiast mounted his camera at a desert water hole using a self-tripping cable release. He got a picture of a kit fox, an animal whose tracks

he had seen at the pond but that he had never witnessed "in person."

Many great wildlife pictures are taken in national parks and wildlife refuges, too, as well as in zoos. If this sort of picture offends the purist in your soul, avoid it. But we all know that some of the nicest wildlife pictures come from poses of semiwild animals. I don't mind these shots. The only offense I take is when the picture is pawned off on me as a shot of a wild animal in the hinterlands when I can see the cement wall of the zoo behind the creature. Parks and zoos may not offer the most authentic wildlife pictures, but they can give us good ones. If you're heading for Yellowstone Park this summer, for example, consider snapping the shutter often.

Sharp pictures occur when the camera is maintained in a steady position. The window pod and tripod help here. Sharpness is also gained through high shutter speed. The blurred picture resulting from camera shake is eliminated with the fast shutter.

There is also an illusion of sharpness related to focus. I took two photos of a sparrow hawk, one with the bird in sharp focus, but with a soft background, the other with both bird and background in sharp focus, lens setting F-11. When I asked friends which bird appeared the sharper, most said that it was the one with background in focus, yet both renditions of the bird were, in fact, equally sharp.

Focus for effect. Try accentuating your subject by opening the lens in order to render the background "unsharp." For other subjects, try using a smaller lens opening, putting subject *and* background in focus. Furthermore, you can gain a sharper photo through camera control. Sit

Lack of light forced an open-lens picture here. Careful focus on the subject, a rest to steady the camera, and a slow shutter release squeeze resulted in a clear photograph.

Safety first. A bison like this one can do a great deal of damage!

down instead of standing, if you can still get the correct perspective of your subject.

Remember that to steady the camera you can use your knees, as well as a unipod in the form of a walking staff. Don't snap the shutter release; depress it slowly and carefully, maintaining the camera as steady as possible all the while.

Patience pays off. If you can wait a photo out, rather than snapping the first image that appears in your viewfinder, you will probably get a better picture. If you stalk close before exposing that frame, you'll probably get a better picture. The impression of stopping flight or animal motion is also worth trying for.

High-speed film allows for that fast, motion-freezing shutter speed. For close pictures of fast-moving birds or animals, a speed of 250th of a second will barely "stop" the action. A speed of 500th of a second, even a 1,000th of a second, may be necessary to freeze action in time. Either move the camera view ahead to where the action is going to be, or follow the view with a smooth, steady swing of the camera, releasing the shutter as steadily as possible. Of course, the motor drive aids greatly in obtaining clear, sharp wildlife action pictures.

Safety first. No matter where you take your wildlife pictures, be careful. Bison, or buffalo as they are popularly called, look about as fast as molasses poured over an ice block and as sharp as the blunt end of a weather balloon. They appear, to sum it up, as a milk cow wearing a fur coat.

Bison, however, happen to be the largest four-footed animal in the North American wild, bigger than a grizzly or a moose, very fast, very powerful. I have watched a bull bison leap a six-foot fence from a stand-still. A buff can turn on a dime and leave you five cents change. Two seasons ago, a visitor to the west wanted his wife to snap a photo of him and a bison in the same frame. This particular bull did not appreciate the invasion of his territory and the tourist was killed for his transgression.

This very season, a photographer died when he came between a grizzly bear mother and a cub he probably had not seen. Wild animals are wild. Treat them with the respect they deserve, even when they are in a national park.

So you have your photos. What to do with them? Wildlife slide shows can be very interesting and handsome. If you really want to be a producer of such shows, take a class from your local college and learn multiple projector use, with sound track.

Photo albums are also very worthwhile.

These are best made from black and white prints, but color slides can be used to make prints if you don't mind the expense. Slides can, of course, be printed in magazines, for fame, money, or both.

Don't pass up the many photo contests around the country—many state conservation magazines hold contests for amateur wildlife photographers. Finally, for those with a serious bent and the willingness to compete with professionals, some publishers will purchase wildlife slides.

RECORDABLE OBSERVATIONS

The wildlife picture itself is the recordable observation of this project. Such pictures can also be a record of animal and bird communication and behavior. If a picture is truly worth a thousand words, there are some photo albums of wildlife in action that are veritable unabridged dictionaries of animal behavior.

CONCLUSION

You will certainly want to take photographs of your subjects when and where appropriate. This brief encounter with the wildlife camera has been meant to launch that picture-taking career.

21

Project Get Close

INTRODUCTION

Action and adventure await when you become a wanderer in the outdoors. Most encounters with wild animals and birds come when you roam far afield on foot — not aimlessly, of course, but without such rigid structure that you must turn a deaf ear to a beckoning fork in the trail. Hiking is a very basic means of seeing wildlife, but getting close is the key to reaping the rewards of each sighting.

There are, of course, many ways to get close to wildlife. We have discussed numerous plans already — the birdhouse, for example, brings wildwatch subjects close for viewing. Taking a stand, building a blind, waiting at a water hole; all of these methods are geared to put wildlife and wildwatcher on common turf.

Project Get Close deals with another form of closing the gap between the naturalist and his subjects — stalking — stalking for the frame-filling picture; the close and accurate observation of wildlife behavior; the thrill of being on the same plane with free-roaming animals and free-flying birds. In stalking, you locate an animal and sneak up on it without being detected.

OBJECT OF THE PROJECT

The object of this project is to get as close as safely possible to the birds and animals encountered on wildlife walks and excursions. Once close, your opportunity for a clear, sharp photograph increases, as do your chances for accurately observing wildlife behavioral patterns. Getting as close as possible is the only way to truly enjoy all aspects of wildlife watching.

EQUIPMENT

Starting at the top, let's talk about the real values of a hat. Many types of hat will keep you warm on your treks afield. Woolen caps, leather caps, insulated hats, hats with ear flaps; the list is almost endless. In order to get close to wildlife, you must first locate wildlife, and that's when a hat *with a brim* comes to the fore.

A brim or visor keeps sun and glare out of your eyes, thereby allowing the pupil to achieve and maintain a reasonable light-gathering dimension. A brim prevents squinting. When squinting, you aren't really looking as carefully as you can for your subjects, because you are uncomfort-

You have to be comfortable in order to enjoy wildlife watching, especially if you are doing a stalk under adverse weather conditions. A good coat is basic equipment during cold weather.

able. Being uncomfortable breaks concentration, and it is often concentration, along with a good dose of patience, that puts birds and animals in your view. By all means, get a hat warm enough for the occasion, but buy one with a brim.

For very cold weather, I like a down coat, such as my Wasatch II model, a very comfortable and effective piece of clothing. Down offers plenty of loft, and loft means that air is trapped and held, forming insulation between the wearer's body and the elements. Down does "puff up," and a down coat is not always without bulk.

For medium weather, the new insulative materials, which are changing names rapidly as chemistry provides better and better substances, offer great warmth without bulk. Thinsulate is one of the more popular and effective man-made materials today.

I like a coat with pockets, and I want the pockets conveniently placed and large enough to hold maps and things. Even in autumn weather, there are cool mornings and afternoons when a hood pulled up over the hat is welcome. Therefore, both of my wildwatch coats, my down model and a Thinsulate model, have attached hoods.

Under the coat, a flannel shirt is nice. Think in terms of layering. As the day warms, it's comfortable to slip the coat off and tie it to the packframe or just carry it; the flannel shirt will provide ample body protection.

Long underwear offers protection on very cold days. Under the flannel shirt, you might want to wear an insulated undershirt. Vests are great for layering, too. A cotton vest works well for early fall; a down vest for late fall and winter. Again, it is the effect of layering that pays off. Woolen pants are excellent for late fall and

The bandanna works in all kinds of weather. It is a sweat band in hot weather, a forehead protector in cold weather, a neckerchief to keep dust out, a mask against blowing dirt, even a scarf over the head for ear warmth.

winter, but I prefer cotton trousers for the early fall, and even shorts for summer wear. If winterwatching, then a fullblown snowmobile suit over regular clothing, along with the down parka, makes a good barrier against the cold.

The bandanna—you know, the kind used by stagecoach robbers in B western films—serves multiple purposes. I have covered my face against blowing dirt on the Yuma desert with a bandanna. I have worn one over my head washerwoman-style to protect cold ears on the winter plains. The bandanna has served as a sweat band around my head in a summer desert, and as a neckerchief as well.

Compact raingear is available in hiking shops. It takes up little space, will fit in a coat pocket, and can make all the difference when the clouds suddenly give up their bounty from overhead.

Boots serve several functions. They protect the feet from sharp objects, water, and cold weather. Therefore, they maintain the hiker's health and safety. I prefer the lightest, least-binding boots that will thwart the elements; however, I'm against the lightweight, soft, clothlike shoe that does not

These American Footwear boots have a quiet sole, and they are waterproof.

protect, even though this very piece of footwear is ideal for stalking.

I was hiking a high desert region in Mexico one year. The friend who accompanied me protested my heavy leather boots. "Why wear things like those in the summer?" he asked. Before that trip was over, my partner had a foot infection caused by a cactus spine.

For most of our wildwatching, a light leather boot with crepe sole will fill the bill. For a great deal of hiking and stalking, an even lighter canvas shoe with a reasonably tough sole will do. Waterproof leather boots, such as those offered by American Footwear, are a wonder in soggy terrain.

The stalker's shoe should be soft-soled, if possible, for the obvious reason of quiet. You see a fox sunning on a rock across a field. There is plenty of cover between you and the beautifully tailed candidate for your camera lens. However, a hard-soled shoe calls out, "Here we come!" on a flat rock, and when you turn the corner, the fox is gone. It happens all the time. Pick a quiet shoe, but be certain it will protect your foot. In wintertime you may wish to select a shoepack—a composite rubber and leather waterproof boot—though I find my American Footwear boots quite waterproof and warm for most of my winter wildwatching.

A smoke bag is nice for stalking. Many

mammals first detect the wildwatcher's presence via his scent carried on the wind. Knowing the direction of the wind, therefore, is often vital for stalking. The smoke bag is simply a small cloth bag, usually with a drawstring, the kind loose cigarette tobacco comes in. The bag is filled with fine, white soot from a fireplace.

In the field, one shake of the bag will put upon the air a fine, soft dust. The dust will mark the currents of air like nothing else I know of. I have often watched the breezes swirl about, knowing of their capricious ways because they could not fool my smoke bag. When making a stalk on a particularly skittish animal, the smoke bag can show which way the wind is blowing, even when the wind is only a gentle breeze caressing your face.

Take binoculars, camera, and notebook along when stalking for close-up views of wildlife. Often, it will be the binocular that shows where the wildlife subject is in the first place. Now that we have compact telescopes and super-light tripods, the scope is also welcomed on the stalking trail. Maps are important, too. The topographical map can lead to excellent wildwatch habitats.

Take a packframe with daypack aboard on the longer treks. The camera's extra lens, film, and many trail items, not to mention food, can be carried via the frame. And don't forget that in wild country where storms may strike without warning, the hiker with mountain tent and sleeping bag tied to his frame is like the turtle—in mere moments he has a shelter against the elements.

METHODS AND PROCEDURES

Trails lead to many wildlife opportunities. Maintained trails, such as those of the

The "smoke bag" is used to test wind direction. This one is a sock with soot in it.

U.S. Forest Service, wind their way into many interesting places off the beaten path, but without the danger of getting lost. You go into the country via a trail, and you come out the same way. Meanwhile, you can spot, stalk, photograph, watch, and enjoy wildlife. I have enjoyed a network of trails in the Bighorn Mountains of my home state. These trails are perfect examples of wildwatching opportunities, where many birds and mammals roam in quiet backcountry, yet there is no problem in getting into and *out of* the area.

While walking, look well ahead and all around in order to spot that candidate for the wildwatch. You will need to watch your footing and use your peripheral vision at the same time. Binoculars are a big help in finding species of interest to study. You must get close, though; that is the focus of this project. Part of getting close has to do

Trying to be a quiet walker is one thing. Being quiet is often another. Moving slowly helps the wildlife watcher who is trying to get close to his subjects.

with fitting into the terrain as a part of it, rather than bumping along like a Brahmin bull at an ice cream social.

Speed of movement is important. Perhaps the grand experts of trailwalking can slip quickly through the undergrowth as quietly as a rabbit, but most of us make more noise the faster we pace. Therefore, slow down. A slow walk is generally a quieter walk. Overraising the boot makes more noise than lifting the foot only high enough to clear obstacles on the path.

The sidewalk shuffle, with toes pointed outward, also tends to be noisy. Practice walking with the toes pointed forward. The tips of your boots will make fewer contacts with brush, rocks, twigs, and other trailwalking obstacles if they point forward instead of out to the side.

Trying to be quiet is one thing; *being* quiet is another. Many of the sounds that are most readily recognizable as human-made come from trailwalkers *trying* to be quiet. The snapping of twigs, scraping of leather boots on rock, brushing of pants against foliage—all of these frighten animals and birds as quickly as the overt crunch of a heavy boot. Most mammals have excellent hearing. You are not going to fool their ears by making tiny stealth-noises in the brush.

If there is no way to be quiet, consider a

better (wider and clearer) trail, or perhaps a higher elevation above the brushlands. Remember, too, that at times it is wiser to stop moving altogether. Walk a little, look a lot.

When a hiker climbs up over a ridge, reaching the topmost part, and just pops over the horizon like a jack-in-the-box, it's called "topping out." In order to get close for pictures or watching, you must top out gently, not all at once. Approaching the horizon, you should stop and peer over the ridge with your binoculars. Move a few more steps, seeing a bit more of the other side, stop, again glass, and then move a few steps, repeating the process. I have oftentimes spotted wildlife over the ridge

that I would have frightened away had I burst into view.

You see a band of deer, antelope, or elk pacing in the distance. Remember that most animals move only far enough away from the point of intrusion as necessary to once again feel safe. Therefore, "cutting them off at the pass" often works. Many times, I have stalked for close observation of moving wildlife by moving ahead and placing myself to intercept the moving animals.

You see an interesting wildwatch candidate in the distance and mount a stalk. First, detect wind direction (using the smoke bag if you have one). Check the direction of the wind continually because

Even though antelope do not seem to use their noses nearly as much as their eyes for detection, moving with the wind in his favor helped the wildwatcher capture this close photo. Note that the buck in the upper center of the picture is beginning to flash the erectile rump hairs as a warning. This is a bachelor herd, all males.

the zephyrs have a habit of changing direction just seconds before you get into position for that wildlife photograph of the year.

Second, determine the lay of the land. Even in seemingly flat terrain, there is usually a watercut, or a few hillocks, or draws, or lumps, or bushes that shield the stalker's approach to close the gap between wildwatcher and wildlife. Use every bit of the terrain to advantage by noting ahead of time where these breaks in the landscape lay.

Also use a frame of reference before hiking off on a stalk. I once spotted a band of javelina in Arizona. A friend wanted close-

The wild turkey is very wary, but he can be approached for good close photos by the careful wildlife photographer. A slow-motion approach helps. Fast movement through the woods causes too much noise.

up photos of the little wild pigs, not that difficult to get, since these near-sighted fellows can be stalked to within mere feet if everything is done correctly. I stayed back, allowing my partner to stalk the sounder of "hogs." He paced downhill, wind in his favor, walking rapidly the first part of the way, and using every bit of terrain to his advantage. One hundred yards before reaching his destination, he swerved, pacing by the animals, which, after catching his scent, raced through the catclaw jungle with a woof! woof! woof! at each bound.

My partner had not taken note of a single landmark to show where the javelina were. Things looked very different once he left the hill we rested on. Down in the valley, the low-level brush was confusing. Had he taken note of a particular boulder, however, one that happened to have a telltale red splotch on it, finding the band would have been easy. The boulder was in sight most of the way. Before departing on a stalk, mark the land ahead visually. Pick out a few features that will be recognizable when you get close to the object of your stalk.

Birds usually cause a bit less trouble for the stalker, but this depends on the birds. I have stalked hawks and eagles by noting a resting ridge, and then coming up to that ridge using brush and boulders to hide my approach. Even though the wind was wrong much of the time, I still got close. I have had a much tougher time getting next to crows and ravens. They are very wary birds; so are wild turkeys. Even the latter rely more on sight and sound than sense of smell.

What about glint and glare, and will smoking alert wildlife? I have no proof that the glint from a packframe has frightened away an animal I was trying to get close to, or that the glare from a wrist-

This antelope took to the trees on a hot day. The photographer was careful to maintain a slow and quiet pace. He also kept pocket change from rattling and his camera from glinting in the sun.

watch has sent a wildwatch species into full flight.

I do know that antelope send messages by flashing the rump patch. Erectile hairs on the whitish rump rise, the sun gleaming from them. These messages are probably read and observed by fellow pronghorns. I have watched the fanny flash in the distance, and by design or accident a whole herd of antelope has cleared out of the valley following that flash. I can't prove the connection between the heliograph rump of the 'lope and the running away of its friends. But to be on the safe side, avoid glints, glimmers, and flashes from your person or gear anyway.

Wildwatchers on stands have noted that the drifting smoke of a cigarette has *not* alerted deer feeding nearby. Since I am not a smoker, I cannot relate any personal experiences on the matter.

I do prevent my gear from rattling along, as I believe that tinny, clanking noises, such as canteens tapping against aluminum packframe struts, do indeed alert wild animals. I have seen this occur several times.

It takes many years of continued and repeated recording of animal behavior to draw strong conclusions. I think, however, that flashes, rattles, and tinkles work against the stalker.

RECORDABLE OBSERVATIONS

Photographs, behavior patterns, added notations on lifelists, and wonderful memories are recorded by the wildlife watcher willing to get close to his subjects. Camera and notebook attend the stalker so that he can record his experiences.

CONCLUSION

You must get close in order to clearly observe and record on film the actions of birds and animals. You do so by taking to trails; by looking for wildlife in the distance; and by careful stalks using stealth, soft-soled shoes where possible, proper clothing and hiking techniques, and even a smoke bag to help you achieve your goal.

22

Project Lurewatch

INTRODUCTION

Some of your best wildlife photographs and notebook entries of wildlife action and interaction may very well result from Project Lurewatch. Bird and mammal activity is often triggered by lures. Learn the ways of lures, and you will become a more proficient wildwatcher. Wild turkeys, crows, ravens, antelope, deer, songbirds, and numerous other species can be lured to the wildlife watcher. Many things may be used for this project, including food, dummies or decoys, scentlures and sightlures.

OBJECT OF THE PROJECT

The object of this project is to employ lures of various types in order to draw wild animals and birds close in for study and photography without harming them. I read of a plan to lure grouse for interesting photographs. Mirrors were placed in the lair of the birds, and cameras were set up to capture the action as the males attacked their own images. The hard mirror was the winner, however, and some of the male birds left the scene of the skirmish a bit worse for wear.

When setting up any sort of lure, ensure that the animal or bird it draws close won't end up battling an unbeatable foe. For example, a cloth dummy of a robin was used to lure male robins during the mating season. Male robins will fight like pit bulls to defend a territory. The soft stuffed decoys, however, did no harm to the gladiators.

EQUIPMENT

There are many commercially prepared lures to choose from. Duck decoys make

From a blind, the wildlife watcher can see many interesting subjects, including waterfowl, which will often decoy into very close range.

superb photographic lures. Operating from a blind, you can take many excellent duck photos, especially with high-speed film and a motorized 35mm camera. Goose decoys are also for sale, some so large that the wildwatcher can crawl inside, his camera aimed through a peephole. Apparently, geese have a little trouble with proportions. To them, these oversized decoys look like the real thing. Of course, that is total speculation. Maybe geese are lured in because they like the big decoys, knowing quite well that they are not geese at all. No matter, the decoys do work.

There are cardboard cutouts and three-dimensional dummies of deer and antelope available. These can be set up in appropriate locales to lure animals of the same species for close-up observation and photography. Owl decoys are also available.

The list of do-it-yourself decoys and lures is limited only by the imagination of the wildwatcher. You can make stuffed "toy" birds and mammals that will lure backyard creatures in close, for example. You can also make cutouts of various creatures, from wild turkeys to deer and antelope, as well as ducks, geese, and shorebirds.

Anise oil serves as a wildlife lure, and many commercial scents are also available. You will also need the old standbys—the notebook and the camera for recording the events that lures present. A tripod-mounted camera with a cable release stationed near a decoy or lure may result in very interesting close-up wildlife photos.

METHODS AND PROCEDURES

There are many ways to lure birds and mammals. Food is one of the more obvious means. In fact, the wildlife garden, wildflower patch, and food stations of various kinds are all lures. Landscaping can also be considered a lure because certain types of vegetation attract animals and birds. Along the lines of food luring is the bait. Patience is very necessary to the success of this wildwatch practice. A bait may draw wildlife to it within hours or it may take days, and some baits never work.

One of the most exciting baits is a livestock casualty. Farmers and ranchers often find a dead sheep, cow, or horse. Transportation is the big problem here. In order to transport large livestock, heavy equipment is needed; a smaller domestic carcass may be transported by pickup truck. Be sure to observe health precautions during such transportation, especially in cases where the cause of death is unknown. This is a very simple and practical approach to luring wildlife.

It is especially practical in regions where large predators and/or omnivorous feeders abound. I sat near a sheep bait in Colorado once that provided me with the most exciting black bear watching I have ever experienced. The project was simple, legal, and totally effective. Its only drawback was photographic—the big male black bear that visited the bait came only at dusk, remaining for a little while into the early hours of darkness, then departing.

Safety—my own—was well planned. I was positioned so the bear could not see me. I was higher than the bait, and the bear's chances of catching my scent were limited. Remembering that, according to some experts, the black bear has attacked more humans than the grizzly, I treated the baiting project with great respect.

A simple stuffed toy can sometimes bring hawks or other predators into close range for study and pictures. It also serves to lure rodents. Be careful to set the decoy up in such a manner that it can be "picked off" cleanly by a bird of prey. Insure that the bird will not be injured while trying to sink its talons into the decoy.

There are dozens of animals that can be attracted to a bait. On a nearby ranch, a horse succumbed to a bad winter. It did not have to be hauled anyplace because it was already stationed perfectly. This "natural" bait drew a long and interesting list of visitors.

Although I never saw a vulture on the carcass, several of these large black birds oftentimes circled overhead. Ravens came in for scraps, usually departing with their victuals to be eaten elsewhere. Coyotes were frequent visitors, mostly at night, but on two occasions were day-spotted feeding away and, incidentally, arguing with each other from time to time. A golden eagle was a latecomer to the dinner party, too,

Food is an excellent decoy in its own right. This desert tortoise remained for a long while feasting on watermelon.

but once it found the feeding site, it spent considerable time dining. I believe the same eagle returned many times to this particular food lure.

Aside from the backyard feeder and the growing garden, there are many other kinds of food lures, including suet, watermelon, bread, vegetables, and spoiled meat. Food lures work well, but only if the time is right. I have deposited the most inviting food lures, only to find them ne-

glected for days on end. Sometimes the lure will go untouched permanently.

A winter-killed antelope carcass behind my home proved to be such an unused natural bait. I dusted around the carcass to see who might be coming to dinner. The guest list was very short — zero. Even though the carcass was in close proximity to civilization, it was, at the same time, on the perimeter of vast ranchland that saw few human visitors and had a good range of wildlife on it, including coyotes. Yet the antelope carcass was never touched.

Decoying is another means of luring wildlife close. The duck decoy attracts because it represents feeding birds. Overhead flyers see the decoys and want to get in on the eating, so down they dive for a closer look, and, quite often, a stopover. If you are there, either concealed in a blind or camouflaged with cover, you will be able to study the birds and photograph their actions.

The goose decoy is also very effective. If a pit is used in conjunction with goose decoys, you stand an even better chance of close observation, along with good action photos and goose portraits. The pit is simply a hole in the ground. It can be as plain as dirt or as elaborate as an underground room, with paneled walls, flooring, and a heater.

From a well-designed and properly positioned pit, the observer can see all around. The goose decoys are set up strategically for the camera. The camera can be mounted on a tripod within the pit, if there is room, and prefocused on the decoys so that the shutter is simply snapped when the big birds are directly over the decoys or amongst the artificial geese themselves.

A bait will serve to bring wildlife in. Bears bait quite well and will sometimes remain in the vicinity until the carcass that lured them is fairly well used up.

Feed can be used in conjunction with such decoys. If you scatter feed around the decoys, the birds that land will stay in the immediate area a good while as they partake of dinner. Their feeding patterns and motions can be observed and recorded. The birds that stop over are in themselves live decoys and may attract a good many more geese.

Dummies are also useful lures. Their level of effectiveness varies widely from species to species, however. I once set out an antelope dummy. Although it drew a lot of visual attention from other antelope in the area, it never attracted one for a close-up look. However, I would still call this dummy a success, because several bands of antelope, seeing the dummy, did move in a lot closer and did remain in the area for a long while. Other dummies, however, can bring more success than I enjoyed with my particular antelope decoy.

A photographer friend brought a series of interesting hawk photos to show me. They were exciting action shots of several different species. Stop-motion shutter speeds had caught the birds in diving flight, with the intent of full attack. The victim of their attack was not in the photograph. "How did you get these photos?" I asked my friend.

"Charlie helped me," he said.

"Another photographer?" I queried.

"No, Charlie the jackrabbit," he said.

Charlie the jackrabbit was a simple stuffed Easter bunny. The wildlife photographer had sprayed the pink toy brown, with masking tape over the inner ears so these areas would remain pink. Charlie was a pretty good-looking jackrabbit, for about two photo sessions. One of the larger hawks became irate when he learned that Charlie was tied down. On his next dive, his sharp talons literally tore the stuffings out of Charlie.

A wild turkey decoy can prove a good lure if the area has sufficient birds in it, especially if the wildlife devotee uses a call in conjunction with the dummy. A rancher friend in South Dakota has a feeding station for wild turkeys. He doesn't need a call to bring the birds in under those circumstances, of course; they arrive on a daily basis, or almost so, for a handout. When he erected his turkey silhouette, it provided no interest at first. The birds, if they took notice at all, glanced and moved on to the feeder—until springtime. Then the fake turkey proved very interesting indeed, especially to tom birds who challenged the dummy's right to be in their territory.

Some animals have a sense of play about them, as we all know. A baby coyote learns many of his hunting tricks through play, and will, in fact, continue to "pretend" most of its life, as will the wolf. The wolf exhibits the same crouching pattern, with forelegs and feet flat on the ground, that we see in our pet dogs when they want us to play with them. This sense of play can make dummies very interesting.

A backyard tree squirrel played a game of "knock the dummy off the fence" as repeatedly as a trained animal might. The squirrel would run out on a tree limb, chattering at the dummy. Then it would make a mad dash down the tree trunk and up the fence post, flying at the dummy. A couple of swift jabs, and the dummy was hurled from its perch on the fence, flying through space and onto the lawn. The attacker would swoop by, jabbing and nipping a few more times before regaining his tree house.

An owl decoy will attract a number of

birds. Although we traditionally think of the owl as luring only crows, I have seen sparrows and other songbirds dart in, all seemingly irate at the audacious owl perched on the tree limb. Interestingly, the very crow that will swoop in to harass the owl will also raise a ruckus over a crow dummy. Crow dummies will attract other birds as well.

Perhaps one of the more humorous incidents in a backyard crow dummy setup was the neighborhood cat who thought itself a very stealthy stalker indeed as it advanced on the black bird perched on the fenceline.

When it caught the bird, however, the cat had the look of surprise of a cartoon feline.

Scent lures should be placed so they carry a long distance on the wind. If the lure is deposited in a lowland hollow that receives little circulation of air, its message may hover there until its potency finally dissipates. The only way the lure will be discovered in this locale is through accident or the good fortune of placing it on a circuit or trailway of a particular animal.

I find that scent, such as anise oil, works well in conjunction with other lures. For

Scentlures will bring animals in close and will often hold their attention for a while. Naturally, these lures work best in areas that are rich in wildlife.

example, when setting a bait out, consider adding to the already inviting aromas of the meal with anise oil or commercial lure.

Study an area well before attempting to use scent lures in it. If you are interested in attracting deer, use scents during the rut. Look for scrapes — elongated channels in the earth scratched out by the buck's hooves — that indicate that the area is in use by rutting deer. Scent may work here.

Look for rubs. These are bare places on small trees where animals have rubbed their antlers, removing some of the bark in the process. These signs are even more important because the buck deer may be de-positing chemical messages on the sapling trees while polishing his antlers. The old notion that the rub was for the purpose of removing "velvet" from the antler, or actually polishing the bony adornment of antlers, has been superceded by the theory that the rub is in fact a biological phenomenon of much greater significance. It is now believed that the rub is associated with the mating cycle, but its exact meaning is yet to be discovered. Find rubs and you know that rutting deer are using the area. Place scents in those regions.

I have lured antelope with a "flag," just a one-foot-square white rag, actually, tied to

A camera on a tripod, with long-range shutter release or remote control operation, will often produce a very nice close-up photo for the wildlife watcher.

Getting close is also a matter of chance. By simply being in the outdoors at the opportune moment, close wildlife photos like this one can be taken. These eastern white-tailed deer allowed the shutterbug an easy picture from a road.

a stick. In many areas, I tried over and over to lure pronghorns without the least bit of success, until on an outing in Arvada, Wyoming, I noticed that several bands of antelope were using a trailway just off Housetop Route, a county road. I placed my flag near that trailway. It seemed to me that since the animals were using that trail on a regular basis anyway, they might condescend to take a closer look at my flag-on-the-stake lure.

They looked, but they never stayed. After a half-hearted glance, the animals would continue on their appointed rounds. After adding a dose of commercial lure to the flag, however, there was considerably

greater interest in the white cloth, and it was not unusual for animals, mainly the bucks, to stand at the flag for a long while inhaling the fragrance of amour. I believe that olfactory lures can be used quite successfully in concert with dummies and at feeding stations to hold the interest of various wildlife subjects.

RECORDABLE OBSERVATIONS

By attaching the camera to a tripod and arranging the setup near any of the lure types mentioned here, you can record your observations through many interesting wildlife pictures. For example, the interesting nighttime pictures of raccoons seen in wildlife magazines often result from food lures in combination with preset cameras. Swift wildlife action can be frozen, too, by preaiming a camera on a specific lure. The high-speed photos of wings of ducks or birds of prey would be very hard to obtain without a lure of one type or another.

There are often a number of actions and interactions you should record in the notebook as well.

CONCLUSION

Lures are created in many different forms; however, the lures central to this project are essentially used to entice animals and birds visually or through the sense of smell. Lures add one more dimension to wildlife watching, a means of enticing animals and birds to come closer for our enjoyment, recorded observations, and photographs.

23

Project Predator Call

INTRODUCTION

Winged as well as four-footed predatory wildlife can be enticed into frame-filling photo range through *calling*. There is nothing new about the art; it dates back to the deepest recesses of the past. Modern predator calling does have a big advantage, however. Numerous over-the-counter commercial calls, instructional tapes and books, and electric cassette calling machines are available today.

The wildlife watcher is able to lure the predator into close proximity through calling because of the nature of the animal. The predator is a hunter—he can also be a bit of a thief. We can assume that the cries produced by calls cause the hawk, owl, coyote, fox, raccoon, and many other predators to come to investigate because they are looking for a free meal, or for an

opportunity to steal away with part of the bounty earned by another predator or at least to partake of the leftovers.

My first experience with predator calling came long before I owned or knew how to use a call. I was hiking in the lower reaches of the Santa Rita Mountains of southern Arizona when a chilling cry reached my ears. I did not know what the noise represented and went to investigate. My mind conjured a picture of a lamb caught in the jaws of a wolf, but there were no sheep where I was hiking, and the last regular wolf sightings in that territory predated my birth. I soon found the source of the cries—a jackrabbit. It was securely caught in a wire fenceline, a foreleg pinned fast.

I had never had a rabbit attack me—but that one acted as if it might. The animal was panic-stricken; when I reached out to help, its ears reared back, and if a rabbit can look fierce, this one did. "Hey, partner," I said, "I'm only going to turn you loose. Take it easy." I got a grip on the ears close to the rabbit's head and began working the leg out of the twisted wire.

Suddenly, something made me look up. An animal was coming. Fast. Right at me. It was a coyote on a dead run. I had not extricated the hare as yet, and the entrance of the coyote on this strange stage of wildlife action broke my concentration. When I let go of its foreleg, the rabbit gave forth once more with its wavering cry. The coyote turned the afterburner on, coming ever faster straight at me.

Wahhhh! Wahhhh! cried the hare. The cause-and-effect relationship here was easy to figure out. The coyote knew full well what a rabbit cry sounded like. The squeal was a call to dinner—a free meal at that. "Hold it!" I said, standing up. The little prairie wolf almost turned himself inside out wheeling around. Dust spewed into the air as the coyote put its gears into reverse. The little wild dog went the other way faster than he had arrived, if possible. I released the jackrabbit, and as it loped away with its crazy gait, I thought about the situation.

The coyote had certainly come to the call of the jackrabbit. Interestingly, when I originally told my jackrabbit-and-coyote story, none of my friends were surprised by it. All of them had either experienced simi-

There is fast action in calling. Here, a coyote dashes into the picture, looking for the entrapped rabbit or hare that it intends to have for a meal.

lar events, or they had at least heard the "death cry" of the rabbit. I was informed that cottontails also made this strange squeal.

I did not become a caller of predators for a long while after that. It was the advent and advertising of the Burnham Brothers predator call that enticed me to give calling a try. I ordered one from the first advertisement I ever saw on the product. The call worked, and it's still working. Only now I have a drawer full of calls, different types for different wildlife and situations.

The art of predator calling can be mastered by any wildlife watcher. Essentially, we are interjecting imitative sounds into the communication patterns of these wild animals. The cry of the rabbit, as well as other auditory pronouncements, communicates to the predator that the rabbit is in trouble, caught in one way or another. The predator investigates to see what he can get out of the situation.

There is more to calling than the basic "I hear a free meal beckoning to me." That has to be true, because in my early calling, I had many odd fellows come to investigate the noise. One afternoon, a sounder of javelina came directly to my squealing. With noses twisting in the wind for information, the little near-sighted porkers walked right into my lap before deciding that I was a human.

All kinds of songbirds also came in. But of the animals that attended my early-day predator concerts, the domestic cow was the strangest guest. Often, cows walked right up to the call. Curiosity? I suppose. I've never known of a cow to devour a rabbit. The predators most often called are coyotes, gray foxes, red foxes, bobcats, and raccoons. Many hawks will investigate a call. One fellow wrote of a hawk trying to

rip the cap off his head as it attacked the cries of the predator call (and caller).

One advantage of predator calling is that it frequently can be done close to home, even in suburban areas. For example, the coyote has managed to set up housekeeping in the suburbs of the city. Los Angeles, Phoenix, and Tucson are just three population centers that report coyote populations within the city limits or nearby environs. Residents of some Michigan cities have also reported coyotes, and these reports are borne out by wildlife experts.

Farms often have foxes and raccoons on the premises. So you can enjoy this project without long-distance travel or large outlays of revenue. Learning to speak this interesting lure-language is not really very difficult. There are rules to follow, but they are simple.

OBJECT OF THE PROJECT

This project serves to introduce you to the art of predator calling. The rewards are close-range sightings of predatory animals and birds for the great memories alone or for recording in written or photographic form. Not only are the sightings close, they can also be exciting. The wildlife generally attracted to these calls—domestic sheep, cattle, farmyard dogs and cats excluded—comes in ready to "duke it out," if necessary, for a meal.

EQUIPMENT

The predator call is, of course, the prime tool for this project. Four of the basic sounds used for the luring of predators are the dying or trapped rabbit, both cottontail and jack; the distressed bird; the howl of the coyote, used only to call coyotes;

A fox is lured into camera range by a Burnham Brothers fox call. It's easy to imagine this fox saying, "Is my meal waiting right over there?"

and the mouse squeak for in-close seduction. There are many other sounds that can be used to attract predators. For example, coyotes have come to turkey calls. The gobble-gobble-gobble was apparently a dinner bell to the coyote. Bobcats have come to duck calls, and so forth. But for the most part, you will speak to predators through the rabbit squeal and mouse squeak.

The tube call is easy to master. I had success with one immediately after listening to a Burnham Brothers instructional record. The tube-type call can be easily varied in pitch, either by replacing the reed or by relocating it within the body of the call. This call is loud, therefore excellent

for long-range work. My Burnham Brothers C-3 Long Range Predator reaches quite far. The body is strong plastic. I have dropped it (and sat on it) with no damage to the unit.

An open-reed call is more versatile than the tube-type unit, although somewhat more difficult to use. It takes longer to master this type of call; those who do can produce a wide range of sounds with one. It is not as loud as the tube-type call but works beautifully in conjunction with the former. Many callers like to wail first on the tube call, for its greater range, switching to the open-reed model after a few moments. The open-reed call is especially excellent when the predator is closing in on the blind. A practiced caller can bring the sound level down to a whisper, without a single sour note.

The diaphragm call has become increasingly popular lately. It is even more versatile than the open-reed model but, again, can take a while to master. There are experts who can call elk, wild turkey, *and* predators, all with one diaphragm call. The diaphragm call leaves hands totally free for camera operation, too. The single-reed diaphragm call gives a high-pitched sound; double- and triple-reed diaphragm calls are lower pitched but very versatile.

There is also the bulb-type call for predators. The one I have imitates the squeak of a mouse. It's very effective when the predator is in sight but will not advance closer to the wildwatcher. The rubber band call is yet another predator-luring device, a rubber band stretched in a holder. It emits a high-pitched moan instead of a squall. It's a good call for close-range use.

Another important piece of equipment for this project is the instructional cassette that can be purchased with the call of your choice. The cassette gives vital specifics in the mastering of the call. It is especially helpful because the newcomer to predator calling can hear a master at work. Mimic this master from the cassette and you're on your way to becoming an expert yourself. I have practiced with the cassette, with unequivocal improvement.

For those who wish the ultimate in calling, the electronic caller or amplified cassette player is available. Burnham Model SC-86 is an example of this unit. The entire outfit comes in one handy nylon padded camouflaged or totally white (for snow country calling) carrying bag with padded straps. The unit is AC or DC operative. After all, some wildlife watchers have predators right in their neighborhoods, so

The open reed call on the left is very good for close-range work. The tube-type call on the right is more often chosen for longer-range calling.

the SC-86 can be set up in the backyard using regular electrical current. The bag contains the tape deck and amplifier, battery charger, speaker, and a fifty-foot speaker cord on a reel for remote positioning, with auxiliary jack for using a nightlight.

The electronic caller can be set up with the speaker fifty feet away from you. This way, the incoming predator directs his attention to the speaker rather than to you, allowing extensive photography opportunities.

Numerous calling tapes are available. Many of the tapes are quite sophisticated and specific—grown jackrabbit calling, juvenile jackrabbit calling, grown cottontail, young cottontail, Yellowhammer woodpecker distress cry, wild turkeys on the roost, cardinal distress cry, the coyote

Today there are many specific calls geared to entice certain species. Try different types to see which work best in your area.

gathering call, quail distress cry, deer cry, and many others.

Olfactory lure is also useful in conjunction with the call as a masking scent. A few drops of commercial scent or anise oil laid out in the probable incoming path of the predator will fool its nose, preventing the animal from detecting your presence through your scent. Mainly, the intent here is masking, so lures that may not serve to attract predators still work well in this application.

A light will be needed for night calling. These may be purchased in various levels of sophistication, from a 1,250,000 candlepower unit with snap-on red lens (quite expensive); to a 400,000 candlepower model, also with red lens attachment, at a modest price; to the ordinary flashlight. Rechargeable models are nice. Be sure to buy spare bulbs, too. Use a red lens, if only a cellophane covering, for night calling.

Another tool for this project is the camouflage outfit. Be certain to match the outfit with the environment—desert colors in the desert; forest colors in the forest. In calling predators, extensive camouflage is a good idea. Predators are very wary and sharp, in spite of the fact that they can be fooled by a squeaking bulb imitating a mouse. Be certain to camouflage your hands, especially if you're fair-skinned. Your hands are going to be in motion when operating the camera, and light-skinned hands in motion are easily detectable.

Also consider using camo tape on your

camera. My cameras are solid black without chrome trim. That means they don't reflect much light, so I do not camo-tape them. Another piece of equipment useful to this project is the portable blind.

METHODS AND PROCEDURES

Find a calling station. As with every project, the habitat comes first. If predators don't frequent the immediate area, you certainly aren't going to call any in. Look for the usual sign—scat, tracks, feeding locales, bedding grounds. For example, I wanted to get a look at a bobcat. I was allowed access to a ranch in northern Wyoming; the rancher had sighted bobcats on several occasions. For a day, I searched for a concentration of sign, finding it near an outcropping of rock. The next day, after I had wailed on the predator call, I had a bobcat twenty feet from me, bristled up like a Fuller brushman's best sample.

Either set up a blind before attempting to call, or ensure that you are well camouflaged and inconspicuous. Essentially, this is taking a stand, so be certain that you can see well, especially in the direction of the most obvious approach. Better yet, situate yourself so that you can see all around. Although it is often possible to determine where the action will come from, you may be surprised. I have had predators arrive from all directions, including a bobcat that poised itself on a rock behind me, watching me make a fool of myself as I bleated

Calls can be so effective that scenes like this may take place. A Burnham Brothers call lured bobcat and coyote simultaneously.

away like an untrained musician on a predator call.

Ready yourself for staying still. Motion will very often destroy success. Remember that even the dim-eyed javelina can quickly detect movement. Try to position yourself so that the wind direction is favorable to the most likely direction of predator approach. Lay out a little masking scent. You are now all set.

First step—do nothing. Let the area "settle down" for a while. You've been on the move and have been heard by the wildlife nearby—count on it. So let the niche rest a minute before you call—make that ten minutes. If calling at night, check your light before blowing notes on your Pied Piper instrument. Ensure that your bulb is intact, your batteries up to power.

Now call. Blow the call, or allow your

Be certain that you are very well hidden when you call. This bobcat cannot locate the caller. If it could, the cat would leave in a second.

electronic caller to work, for about thirty seconds. Then allow twice that amount of time for silence. Then give it another thirty seconds, and another moment of silence. Groan, moan, quaver the voice of the call. Call with feeling. When I was first given that advice, I chuckled. "Play it again, Sam, with feeling," I teased. But my mentor was right.

I invented my own way of creating intensity in the call—imagination. I imagined that first jackrabbit I found so long ago entangled in the fenceline. Then it was easy to get the right tone into the call. Listen to your instructional cassette. Good callers have that "feeling" of intensity.

Switching calls is a good idea. I use a tube-type long-range call for starters, changing to the close-range unit after a couple of tries with the louder call. This change is effective. I have also used the jackrabbit distress cry followed by a coyote call when trying to lure the desert canines into close view. If a predator responds to your initial bleats, and if it is coming straight into your hideout, don't give your position away. And switch calls, going for the close-range type.

Suppose that there in front of you stands a fox. He's been called in, but he's still 100 yards away. You switch from a long-range to a short-range call; the fox responds by moving closer, but he's still too far for close observation or photos. Now use the bulb squeaker. Don't overdo it. If the fox doesn't advance for the mouse squeak, he probably isn't going to come in any closer.

If nothing happens for a half hour, move to another spot. Chances are the predators simply aren't interested in your call, or there aren't any close enough to hear it. Start over—a brand-new spot, a little masking scent, use of the long-range call, then the short-range call.

If hawks take interest, but move away before getting very close, your overhead camouflage is probably lacking. If predators advance on your blind, but dart off from fairly long distance, there may be something amiss with the location of your masking scent, or your blind or camouflage may be inadequate.

RECORDABLE OBSERVATIONS

The obvious record of predator calling is a photograph. I confess that my personal interest in predator calling is not, however, in the picture; I like the memory-making thrill of it. Incoming predators can be pretty worked up, excited, if I dare make an anthropomorphic comment, happy, and very animated—yet wary and cautious, all at once. So I record wildwatch memories more than photos. You may wish, however, to make a specific photo file just for calling. Some of the recorded sequences will be startling.

Written reports are also valuable in predator calling. There are, perhaps, more interesting stories connected with calling than with any other wildwatch project. Once I had coyotes arriving from three different directions simultaneously, and timed to arrive at my blind within seconds of each other. I switched to the squeaker as they approached, and all three came to a stop, ears set as homing devices.

I called again. The three animals, only a few feet apart in a small clearing in front of my stand, caught sight of each other. They sat down. They looked at each other. No

Look hard. That is an African lioness in the center, lured in with a tube-type varmint call.

matter how much squeaking I did, the coyotes paid attention only to each other for a couple of minutes, then they left. This was typical of wild animal behavior, and I never deciphered their motives. There was no tussle, not even a verbal argument. The little wild dogs simply elected to leave a "free meal" behind.

Predator calling can result in swift action, and action makes for good notebook fodder, as well as fine photos. A lifelist of called predators will contain many action entries, while at the same time offering an interesting collection of data concerning wild animal behavior, action, and interaction. Night calling has its own special brand of excitement, too. As always, respect the animals you are enticing. You may be expecting the approach of a little fox when a big bear shows up. Be like the Boy Scouts—prepared for all events.

CONCLUSION

Predator calling is one more tool in the kit of the complete wildwatcher. You may begin this project as a novice, but with the proper instructional materials and practice, chances are an expert caller will emerge in only a few weeks of concentrated effort.

Be cautious. Most predators, such as the fox or coyote, will not harm you, but the predator call could lure bears or other more dangerous animals. Be sure that you have a good view of the calling area, and if a large predator comes in, be prepared to retreat to safety.

24

Project Birdcall

INTRODUCTION

Many nonpredatory birds can be lured into our circle of wildwatching through calling. This project is concerned with calling songbirds, quail, crows and ravens, ducks, geese, and wild turkeys. Pay special attention to the warnings below pertaining to calling songbirds during mating or nesting cycles. Calling birds works so well that we can, under certain circumstances, seriously upset the balance of their life cycles.

OBJECT OF THE PROJECT

The major objectives of Project Birdcall are learning to use bird calls and various other methods of birdcalling and doing so without harm to the birds that respond to our auditory lures.

EQUIPMENT

Bird calls, primarily commercial models, plus a tape machine, are necessary for this project, although there are many expert birdcallers who have learned to call birds without the aid of commercial calls or cassette tape machines. An electronic caller of high volume, such as the Burnham Model SC-86, will do the job even better, but a smaller recorder will suffice in most neighborhood or city park areas.

For songbirds, calls can be made in two ways, by using the human voice and by using the tape recorder. You may wish to purchase a specific call designed to entice quail. They also will respond to the open-reed varmint call and the diaphragm call. I have had success with the Burnham Model Q5 quail call. Its cost is under $7.

Most calls are quite easy to use. This One-Hander is a very good example of a fine turkey call that can be mastered with a few quick lessons and some practice.

Crows and ravens respond well to a call under many conditions, especially in barnyard areas where they have been allowed free access to food; however, there are tapes that work as well or better than the tube-type crow call. The plastic tube-type crow call is extremely portable and can be very effective in many areas. The tube-type call I have can be operated without the hands, leaving you free to use a camera.

Neither a duck call nor a goose call needs to be expensive. There are, to be sure, many high-class duck and goose calls, some of them collector's items in their own right, and very expensive; however, you can do a fine job of luring waterfowl in for close observation and pictures with the basic calls available in the $15-or-under bracket.

Wild turkeys can be lured in close with many different types of calls. There is the

basic slate and dowel model, used with blackboard chalk, which costs under $10. The basic model of the diaphragm turkey call may be purchased for only $4; the more expensive diaphragm turkey calls cost $5 or $6.

The model I use is the box-type call. I like it best because it works so easily and so well for me and because it sells for less than $10. These cedar boxes produce great tones, from the gentle cluck of the hen to the rasping gobble of the mate-seeking tombird.

Audio cassettes are extremely useful for luring birds. There are many to choose from. My particular listing includes a cardinal distress cry; a flicker call; a woodpecker call; a cardinal call; a meadowlark call; a quail call; an owl and crow fight (used to lure crows and ravens); crows calling in singles and groups; a hooting owl; a mallard duck feeding and quacking; a flock of geese "talking" plus a flock of geese feeding, with the particular goose conversation that feeding Canada geese employ; wild turkeys on the roost; a wild turkey gobbler calling for a fight; a spring turkey hen; a turkey hen talking, with gobblers answering; a strutting turkey gobbler answering hen calls; and many more. All of these and other recorded cassettes make excellent auditory lures for wildwatchers.

The camera is, of course, an integral part of this project, as is the notebook. Many birdwatchers use calls and/or cassettes to gain sightings of birds they may never see otherwise, thus adding appreciably to their lifelists. One of the more interesting aspects of this project is keeping the wildlife journal, because birdcalling often evokes considerable interaction among other animals as well as winged incomers to the calls.

Binoculars are also very useful. Use

them not only to identify species for a life-list, but also to help you make note of bird and animal behavior, which may otherwise be missed or misinterpreted from a distance.

METHODS AND PROCEDURES

Songbirds are lured to the wildwatcher mainly because of their mobbing instinct. The birds tend to "gang up" on intruders of various types, from birds of prey to neighborhood cats. Perhaps they are trying to create confusion; it is common for little "backyard birds," especially pas-serines, to congregate when another bird is in trouble. They cause a terrific ruckus, flying about the foe like animated darts; and though they can do no real damage, they often annoy the aggressor to the point of its leaving the area, even a predator many times their size.

You can effectively imitate the alarm call of passerines by noisily "kissing" the knuckles of your hand, either open or closed in a fist. A click! click! click! sound results, similar to the noise humans make when calling Priscilla Pussycat to dinner, only louder and with more intensity. The noise is prolonged and continuous. This

Songbirds have a whole vocabulary in their "music." Wildlife students are just now unraveling some of these vocal mysteries.

alarm cry usually does the trick, though admittedly some callers are better than others in creating a realistic call. If the call is a high-pitched, squealing sound, it seems to evoke the desired sound better than a low-pitched sound. This call mimics the cry of a bird caught in the clutches of a sparrowhawk, tomcat, or other predator.

I heard this call no more than three feet from my head one day. I was on the campus of the University of Arizona when a high-pitched sound burst from the branches of a tree. A sparrowhawk had caught a sparrow. The smaller bird was pinned under the talons of the larger bird. But the tiny hawk could not finish the job, and the little bird soon had help in the form of mobbers all around. The hawk let

Taped territorial calls can bring in a variety of birds. Naturalists are still studying the meaning of these songs. Many of the findings are fascinating.

go, and the sparrow flew away as if the devil itself were on its tail.

I have never been able to copy that sound; however, even my poor rendition of the "passerine opera" has enticed birds to fly in for a look at the supposed intruder molesting one of their ilk.

Use a tape recorder to capture the sound of real mobbing birds. Set a decoy on the branch of a tree—a pretend owl will do—and give forth with the alarm cry. Have a tape recorder going in close proximity to the decoy. If things go right (they may not at first, so try again), you will have a tape of a passerine gang raising a ruckus with an intruder. Then the tape can be used to entice other birds for wildwatching.

There are commercial tapes that serve the same purpose. A cassette of the screech owl can bring a great many smaller birds into the area, for example, so can the sounds of a scolding wren.

Taped territorial calls can also bring response from nearby birds. However, *do not call* in the springtime when nesting is in progress or during the height of the mating cycle. Such alarms may cause nesting or mating birds to leave their duties for good. The obvious result is fewer songbirds.

The alarm cry has also been known to deter songbirds from feeding, interrupting their feeding patterns. During late summer, such interruptions won't cause a serious problem. The birds go back to their business soon enough. In cold winter months, when the birds must ingest large quantities of food to keep their body temperatures up, a cessation in feeding may bring serious consequences.

Quail can be called in for close observation by using an imitation of the assembly. Chi-qui-ta! Chi-qui-ta! You have heard this sound even if you do not live in quail country, for it is often used as a back-

These ravens respond to a crow call. All of the reasons for birds coming in to a particular call are not known.

ground theme in western movies. I have called only the quail of the Southwest. My method is simple.

I have always situated myself in a wash — a dry waterway — for quail calling. Hunker down in the brush, but on a rise so that you can see all around the wash. Call. Call again. And again. Best results occur in early morning and late afternoon. The quail will assemble right in front of you if your call is true. The commercial quail call is excellent. I used one in late afternoon to call the local quail in practically like pets to the waterhole and feeder. A few chi-qui-tas! and the birds would soon arrive at our backyard.

Crows and ravens also respond to a call. Use an owl decoy in conjunction with calling; or better yet, use an owl and crow decoy set, placing crow decoys on the ground as if they were feeding, as well as in nearby trees. Best results will occur on a flyway coming from a roost, but even if you know where the roost is, leave it alone. Once you disturb the roost, your wild-watch birds may leave for another region.

Avoid being seen by the sentinel crow. He is usually the first arrival to your call. If that crow spots you, it will return to the flock with bad tidings. Don't even try to photograph that first bird; stay put in your blind and allow him to look things over and depart without knowledge of your presence. The sentinel crow, it is believed, flies ahead of the flock to investigate the situation for the rest of the band.

I have found that a truer sound is produced by placing the mouthpiece of the call fully into the mouth, rather than pursing the lips over the end of the call. The tube-type crow call has a slit in it. If the slit is not encompassed, air passes through it, reducing the effectiveness of the call. This slit is functional. By lightly biting down with the teeth to depress the slit, the tone of the call changes. The sound rises in pitch as the slit is clamped shut.

I cup my hands around the opposite end of the call, producing a muffled, but not necessarily subdued, sound. Caw! Caw! Caw! The sound "bouncing" from cupped hands seems to be truer and more realistic. Hand posture can alter the sound of the crow call considerably. I learned that, with a predator call, it was wise to cup the hands almost closed over the end of the call initially, opening them slowly as the volume increased. But with the crow call, keep your hands in a cupped posture. This makes the caw! caw! sound uniform.

Crows are as wary a bird as can be imagined and as elusive as the wild turkey. Studies of crows reveal a high level of avian intelligence. Crows quickly learn to do tricks, for example, and they also learn simple puzzles rather rapidly when required to for procurement of food. Expecting the crow (or its larger cousin, the raven) to swarm around you like bees at the hive as you stand in the middle of a field serenading them with your little call is folly. If ever you put camouflage and concealment to work, do so in crow calling, and use a portable blind where practical. I have never lured a crow or raven close by standing in the open while calling.

Tandem crow calling is best. As few as two callers can produce sounds that imitate a flock of birds. One caller cannot do this, because there are never two simultaneous caw! caws! and the birds detect that fact. Your wildwatch partner and you, however, can present flock sounds together. If you wish to become an expert crow caller, listen to their language. Crow calls have been broken down into several communications, including the feeding call, the rally call, the discovery call, the distress call, and the call given by very young birds.

Ducks are lured to the call to congregate as well as to feed. Although calling without benefit of decoys is successful in some regions (I found a hot water spring and swampy area in Idaho that produced excellent calling results without the use of decoys), the interested birds expect to see their calling cousins below, frolicking in the water and having a wonderful time. When they look down and see no other birds, they usually continue flying. Therefore, duck calling is best accomplished in conjunction with decoys. It is not easy. I have never mastered the duck call because of lack of practice.

To become expert in duck calling requires that you learn the various ducks and their many calls. One given type of duck may have numerous patterns of speech. Generally speaking, there is the quacking, murmuring, and chattering of the surface-feeding duck; the burr-burr-burr of diving ducks (in various pitches); feeder calls; and come-back calls in many variations.

The dedicated duck caller knows his birds and their individual language. He may use binoculars to identify overhead ducks before trying to lure them with his call. Look at it this way: If you were trying to communicate to a non-English-speaking person in your native tongue, you'd get nowhere fast. You will reach the same destination speaking to diver ducks in surface duck speech.

Get a good cassette and learn to imitate the calling patterns of the ducks in your region. Practice these calls, and listen to ducks in the wild so that you can add to your knowledge. Use a blind or strict camouflage if you expect ducks to pose for your camera. Ducks seem to be able to see an uncovered human thumbnail at 100 paces. If you've been in a small airplane or helicopter at low altitude, you may have seen the upturned faces of people below.

When a person looks up, especially if he has a light complexion, his face acts as a heliograph, sending a flash skyward. Cover or camouflage your face before attempting to call ducks close.

Goose calling is a bit easier. There are mainly low-pitched calls of the Canada goose and higher-pitched calls of the lesser Canada, snow, specklebelly, white front, and blue goose. Again, calling coupled with decoys works best, and a blind or total camouflage is needed.

In winter, when you are calling over a snowfield, covering up with a white sheet works well, provided movement is held to a

The box-type turkey call gives excellent tone and a wide range of sounds when the wildwatcher learns how to gain the most from it.

minimum. A few wiggles and even a sheet-covered wildlife watcher will be detected by any respectable goose. The full-blown pit offers best cover, and also best comfort, along with an excellent shelter for both you and your camera. The camera can be pre-located so that the simple tripping of the shutter will freeze the action of incoming geese.

Wild turkeys are not necessarily clever. They are very wary, however, and they have several attributes working for them: fine eyesight, excellent hearing, and natural suspicion of anything that looks out of place in their environment. I do not believe that wild turkeys detect our presence by scent; however, the birds can *see* the slightest movement. Before attempting any turkey calling, find a good shelter in which to conceal yourself while being able to see out clearly for observation and photos. Wear camouflage, and stay still.

Using the box-type turkey call, make the "cluck" sound by lifting the lid and tapping the hinged end with a forefinger. The cluck seems to communicate "Come this way. I have located something interesting, something to eat." Use this call as a general "feeler" to see if you can interest a bird in answering. If your cluck! cluck! turns into

Remember that you can lure birds of prey with predator calls. An owl like this one feeds on cottontail rabbits and can be enticed to come to a rabbit distress cry.

a full-fledged putt! putt! you may send your birds running, for that's the danger call. Don't overdo your response to any turkey reply. Chances are if you work too hard at it, the incoming birds will end up going the other way. The cluck, cluck call can be used at any time of the year.

The "yelp" is best used in the springtime, during the mating season, because it is the mating invitation of the young henbird. If you master this sound, you may need no other. This call usually comes in threes, and it is high-pitched. Space each yelp by the count of two — yelp (one by one thousand, one by one thousand) yelp! (one by one thousand, one by one thousand) yelp!

The famous gobble! gobble! gobble! is also useful during the mating season. It's the calling card of the tombird, of course, and should you get an answer, talk only when he talks. You can literally send the bird the other way by overdoing your gobbling.

If you hear turkeys and wish to call them in, imitate only the sounds that the birds make. A big mistake is making turkey talk that does not fit in with the time of year or circumstance. Mating calls in the middle of summer are out of place, for example, and will oftentimes repel the birds from the caller.

Do obtain and listen to an instructional cassette on turkey calling. Practice the language until you can "talk turkey" with effectiveness. The expert turkey caller puts real feeling into his yelps, the most important word in wild turkey language.

RECORDABLE OBSERVATIONS

Record the behaviors you have observed through birdcalling with both photographs and notes. Because calling sometimes brings in those species that have not been encountered before, lifelists can be greatly enhanced by birdcalling.

CONCLUSION

There is no way to describe all the different languages of various birds. Fortunately, cassettes are available to teach us the speech patterns of many species, or to be played through tape machines for those who do not wish to learn the art of calling. Through practice, you can speak to many different birds, coaxing them in close for observation and photography. The wildwatcher who employs no calling methods at all is ignoring a significant aspect of wildlife enjoyment and study.

25

Project Territory Call

INTRODUCTION

This project deals specifically with calling animals that are responding to a territorial imperative. These animals are defending or establishing a territory for the purpose of mating. That makes the entire atmosphere of the calling different. When a coyote has been lured to a prospective meal by the distress cry of a rabbit, he is not necessarily willing to fight when he arrives on the scene. But a bull elk, who is defending his territory, is. He is not coming in for a mouthful of grass, but rather to lock antlers with an antagonist for the right to a harem of cows. Therefore, this project is quite different from the previous calling project because we are interested in different subjects who are responding to the call for a different reason.

Even though elk and moose are not near-to-town subjects of wildlife study, I am including them because these animals lend themselves nicely to wildwatching. They can be seen, not only in the wilderness, but also in national parks (such as Yellowstone Park) as well as in many open-air zoos. Maine has a strong population of moose; Colorado and Wyoming have many elk; and there are many other excellent areas for both.

The other animals dealt with in this wildlife-calling project are the javelina — somewhat rare, but an interesting animal for those living in the Southwest — the deer, white-tailed, mule, and blacktail, and of course, the squirrel, dweller of numerous near-to-city forests and resident of many backyards in North America. You need not travel to the backcountry to find deer and squirrels, and you would be surprised if you knew how many larger quadrupeds live in close proximity to your homes. I have left out bears, in spite of the fact that black bears have been called many times. Commercial black bear calls are not available.

Before attempting to call any of the larger mammals, plan for your safety. Don't get into the forest, wail on your call without discretion, and then be surprised when a mountain lion shows up with fury in its eye.

My own son John had a mountain lion experience he will not soon forget. He was wildwatching in the Rockies when a big cat came along with her kittens. The youngsters insisted on walking behind John, putting him in between Mom and them. The mountain lion became very upset over the whole matter and showed it. John backed away and finally worked himself out of the immediate reach of the cat.

In areas where bears reside, keep in mind that you may call one in. Dangerous? The black bear is considered a clown of the woods — except by the people who have met an angry one. Mountain lions, too, are deemed wary creatures that run the other way. They are wary, and they do run the other way, *most* of the time. Use discretion. Be cautious. Wildwatching is a safe hobby. Keep it that way through preplanning. Call only from a position with a good view. If an animal comes along that you don't want to deal with, have a ready exit.

OBJECT OF THE PROJECT

The object of this project is to employ calls designed to entice various animals into camera and close observation range. The animals of interest for our project are deer, elk, moose, javelina, and tree squirrels.

EQUIPMENT

The Burnham Brothers D-4 deer bleat call is one of the better units for calling deer. It currently sells for under $10. There is also the buck snort call, as well as the newer buck grunt call and the antler-rattling kit. I have used predator calls that attracted deer and javelina.

There are numerous elk calls on the market. The newer elk cow call is highly thought of, as are many of the diaphragm models and the older (but excellent) whistle.

Moose calling, touched on here for the benefit of those of you from Maine, Idaho, Utah, Wyoming, Canada, plus national park visitors from all over the country, can be accomplished with a homemade birch-bark horn.

There are many squirrel calls that imitate the barking of the bushytail. You may also carry two quarters in your pocket for this project. I have called squirrels into picture-taking range with such pocket change.

The standby 35mm camera, the binocular, and the notebook are indispensable for this project. Also carry some commercial liquid lure, anise oil, or masking essence.

There are many excellent videos of elk-calling for rent that have been reviewed with high praise for their accuracy. I reviewed three elk-calling tapes recently and found all of them to be highly informative, and the video tape is an excellent teaching tool.

METHODS AND PROCEDURES

Deer calling should be considered by all wildwatchers because the great majority of us have deer relatively close to home. A family outing in many public land areas

This deer call resembles a bleating sound. The author used one on an outing and called in numerous white-tailed does.

may bring close encounters with the deer family, especially if you know how to call these interesting animals in for observation.

I have had many mixed adventures in deer calling. On one trip into the Whetstone Mountains near the Arizona/Mexico border, a companion, Ted Walter, and I called literally dozens of desert whitetails in rapid succession. They were all does. They all came on a dead run, with what seemed to be great curiosity in their eyes. They stamped their feet, marched right up to our concealment, and, even after we stood up, stayed for a moment.

I called several buck deer on a desert camping trip a year later. Now, instead of does coming to the call, only bucks came in. They, too, approached as if they were curious about the bleating. They, too, departed slowly even after seeing a human standing up in plain sight. Again, I used the bleating-type call, a tube-type plastic unit. If you are interested in calling deer, you must, as I have said before, choose the right locale. Scrapes and rubs in an area denote mating season interest, for example, and are good choices of area. I have also called deer in midsummer, locating good habitat by checking for the usual sign—droppings, tracks, plant use, and so forth.

In deer calling, select a blind or remain out of sight by using natural cover in the terrain. Camouflage is again of great importance. A face mask is useful, especially if you have to rise above your concealment to snap a photo. Lay down a little scent in a circle around your blind . . . a few drops here, a few drops there. Two kinds of lure are useful: anything that will mask the scent of the wildwatcher, from apple aroma to skunk essence, and the liquid lures that mask human odor *and* invite deer at the same time. As a seasoned

wildwatcher now, you know how you are going to be detected by a deer—he's going to sniff you out (so the scent is an excellent block to that problem), or he will sight movement. So don't make overt gestures; move very slowly and stay down. Remain camouflaged, using brush and natural depressions in the ground to hide your form.

Seasonal timing is important in terms of mating season vs nonmating season. I have, however, called deer in the middle of the summer (at midday, too). The best time of day for deer calling is during their periods of greatest activity, early morning, late afternoon, and nighttime. I have

Cup the hands about the call to muffle the sound. Then open the hands toward the end of the bleat. Hand motion can considerably alter the sounds of a call like this.

called some beautiful deer at night in the cold of winter, but I gave the practice up. The deer were visible only by flashlight, and the sightings never produced a good photo, or any interesting behavior patterns.

There are several types of deer call. The plastic tube call produces a distress cry or a bleat (a sort of bawl). Deer tend to investigate these noises. When using the tube call, cup your hands about the unit completely, and begin with a strong call. Blow very hard, slowly opening the hand. Really raise a fuss on the call, create a ruckus, lots of commotion. Do this six to a dozen

times, then be silent. Sit very still, and cupping your hands about your ears, turn slowly to pick up sound. You may hear your deer coming in.

On your second series of calls, again close your hand around the end of the deer call, but don't blow so hard this time. Make three to six bleats, each about two seconds long. Stop, look, listen. Continue this process for fifteen to twenty minutes on a stand. Then move on. If it is mating season, try the deer grunt call. If a buck deer is sighted during the mating season, but will not come closer, try the grunt call. The commercial buck grunt call is a plastic

A grunt-type deer call can bring a buck like this in for a look. Deer make a number of sounds that are associated with the territorial imperative.

tube-type unit with a plastic tube connected to the outlet of the call.

The grunt-type call should be used in conjunction with other calls, especially when rattling antlers to lure bucks in during rut. Use it sparingly. The grunt call entices the rutting buck to come forth and do battle and works only during the rut. Look for scrapes and rubs in the area before trying the call, or use it only when you know a buck is near but will not come in. Grunt with one or two short bursts, then stop and wait.

The use of shed antlers comprises another deer call. The antlers are rapped together to imitate the fighting of two rival bucks during the rut. They are also used to thrash nearby brush, suggesting a buck ready to defend his territory. If you do not wish to bother with deer antlers, there is now a commercial item for sale called a "rattling sack." The nylon sack is held between the hands and shaken, producing its antler-clashing noises with hard hickory sticks.

Elk are not that difficult to lure by call, provided the rut is in full swing and there are bulls in the immediate area to hear your call. The ordinary "elk whistle" sound will carry a mile on quiet days; however, enticing a bull elk to come a full mile to the caller is not too likely.

The use of the newer cow call interested me; it can bring remarkable results. The diaphragm, especially in conjunction with a grunt tube, seems to produce a very accurate bull bugle; remember, though, the diaphragm-type calls require practice for perfection.

There are three major elk-calling techniques. First is to call minimally. Let the bull do most of the talking. Give a whistle or two, followed by the appropriate grunts,

and then if a bull does answer, return his call sparingly.

The second method is quite the opposite. Here, the caller takes command. He raises a ruckus on the elk bugle, challenging all bulls in the area to come forth to do honorable battle for the fair damsels.

Third, there is tandem calling, a method already mentioned in luring crows. Two callers spaced apart can sound like rival bull elk, which in turn may entice a third party—the real bull—to come and take a look at the combatants.

Sunrise is a good time for calling, although I have heard the odd call of the bull elk at all hours of the day, especially late afternoon. Again, the blind or some form of hideout is necessary, because the elk, even when it's on the prod, can detect movement and human presence in a heartbeat.

The nose of the elk is typically acute. He can tell your brand of aftershave from a half mile, so lures, masking scents mainly, should be applied in the immediate calling area. It is also useful, at times, to thrash the brush vigorously with a dead branch as if antlers were flogging the foliage, as well as to rake the ground with the same branch in simulation of hoof-pawing.

I have been in Yellowstone Park during the elk rut. The sound cannot be fully described; however, the uh-wheee! —uh— ugh!-ugh!-ugh! seems not to belong to the mighty bull elk, but rather to some form of bird. The rutting bull is seeking its harem or trying to retain it. Coughing, braying, and whistling, with a little end-of-call grunting, are actually not too difficult to imitate with practice.

The moose is another of the big mammals that won't be seen all that often by very many of us, but he can be called.

The bull elk emits a sound incongruous with its large size. This call is often termed a "whistle." Modern elk calls are better than ever. They now include a cow call as well as the "elk bugle."

Moose are exciting animals to entice in. I have a small population of moose only ninety minutes from my doorstep, and when they "get riled," watch out. The moose call, some say, imitates the call of a bull looking for a fight. I think it's a cow looking for something else. Along with grunting into the "megaphone," which is all the birchbark tube really is, the caller makes an uh-wahh! uh-wahh! sound. He may also rake the brush, snap twigs, and

scrape trees in simulation of antler-polishing and thrashing of vegetation. Hackles raised and eyes all but rolled back into their sockets, a bull on a prod is a real sight to behold.

The little javelina of the Southwest is closer to a great number of wildwatchers than many naturalists realize. Texas and Arizona have good numbers of wild pigs. New Mexico also carries a reasonable wild pig population. Therefore, ignoring these little porkers is allowing a possible wild-watch experience to drop by the wayside.

I have no special javelina call. The animals I have called in have all responded to my regular predator call. The tenets of good calling were observed—good javelina habitat, a correct calling site, and sufficient cover to obscure the caller, but I haven't taken pains to camouflage myself. Setting out masking scent would be a good idea, though I generally bypass that, too.

I've taken to a higher ridge in my calling, keeping my scent well above the ground. Using binoculars, I sight the little pigs on their way in. Their behavior has always been interesting to me. I once watched one of the "hog party" become irate about my calling, at which he (or she—it's hard to tell which is which) took a nip at a partner, and a short scuffle ensued. Nobody was hurt.

Squirrel calling is perhaps not calling after all. At least I can lay no claims to having lured a bushytail from a distant tree to my side. I have, however, gotten many a good, long look and a terrific conversation with tree squirrels by using a call. Current commercial squirrel calls are the best ever. I just bought, for under $5, a squeeze call that imitates the bark of the tree squirrel. It sounds quite good to my ear, and it must sound pretty good to bushytail, too, because it has lured several to hang around a while longer. My own method of using the call is as follows.

Pace the squirrel's habitat slowly. Sim-

The moose may also be called during its mating season. Use caution. A bull moose on the rampage is a very formidable animal.

The javelina, a little "wild pig" of the Southwest and Mexico, will also come to a call. The author has called several sounders of javelina with an ordinary predator call imitating the distress cry of a rabbit or hare.

ply enjoy the stroll. When a squirrel is sighted on the ground, move to it immediately. The squirrel will tree, hopefully before running a long distance. Squirrels are not too fleet of foot anyway, so you can generally catch up with one quickly. When the squirrel trees, then use the call. Oftentimes, the little rascal will pop out and give you a scolding in squirrel language that would probably be censured.

Employ the same simple tactic when a squirrel is sighted in a tree. See if you can't get the fellow to converse with you, perhaps stepping out on a limb in full view as he scolds and orates.

If you don't happen to have a squirrel call handy, two quarters will often do the trick. Place one quarter in the palm of your left hand if you are right-handed. With the other quarter, tap as rapidly as you can against the palmed quarter. This little trick somewhat duplicates the chattering sound of a barking, scolding squirrel. It apparently sounds pretty good to them.

A short time ago, I was trying to get a squirrel to come down from the density of a high tree, just a little lower into less foliated branches so I could have a little chat with him and take a good look at the fellow. I tried the quarter-tapping trick and down he came. I did have my camera along; I now have his portrait.

RECORDABLE OBSERVATIONS

Perhaps the most interesting aspect of calling is notekeeping. At least as important as a photograph, the events of calling deer, elk, even squirrels, are generally behavioral in nature. I've had the smallest squirrel react with indignity at my calling him down from his tree into full view.

Javelina have done some very interesting things when called. One of the biggest insults I've suffered in calling came at the hand of a little wild pig band. I called the group to handshake closeness. And then, in the midst of my best concert, the entire sounder, about a dozen strong, ceased all interest in my music and began to feed on prickly pear fruit.

Of course, the wildlife photo taken on a calling trip has great potential, too, because the animals that do come in are often alert, and they look it. They look interested, and, therefore, are interesting. They show personality traits not necessarily seen if you have just happened upon them at rest or during feeding. A feeding deer is one thing; a deer charging into a call of any sort is quite another. Also, as in calling any wildlife, the luring of quadrupeds can help

Wildlife photos of called animals are often exciting because the animals themselves are animated. These bucks responded to a call even though it wasn't mating season.

One false move and the called animal is gone. Be aware of wind direction and remain well hidden during the calling sequence. Although called animals often throw caution to the wind when they respond, this does not mean they are oblivious to an obvious human form or the disturbing scent of man.

build a lifelist. There are some animals that one may not see closely but for a call.

CONCLUSION

All forms of wildlife calling are interesting. While the opportunity for calling some of our quadrupeds is admittedly limited, this does not make the pursuit less worthwhile. Even though I have a moose population no more than one and one-half hours west of my home, I see only a few of these huge animals annually, and I've called but few of them. Nonetheless, the experiences that I have had with moose have been worthwhile. I have enjoyed them and also have enjoyed taking their portraits.

Carry a deer call on your next foray into whitetail, mule deer, or blacktail country. Try to get the attention of squirrels with a call or the coin trick. If you have a chance to enjoy wildlife out west, consider elk calling if the time of year is right for it. Be a wildlife caller.

A Lifetime of
Wildlife Watching

Wildwatching is self-perpetuating. Curiosity calls and is answered, but the answer circles back upon itself, and again we are curious. So again we look and again we ask why. A new sense of awareness develops. We understand nature better; we appreciate her more. Soon the hobby of wildlife watching becomes a lifestyle, and the lifestyle is passed on to our young wildlife watchers. They hold it for a lifetime, too, and, we hope, share it with others.

Index